PATRICIA BOYER WEISMAN

SCORNED

 WorkBook

WORKBOOK PRESS LLC
187 E Warm Springs Rd,
Suite B285, Las Vegas, NV 89119, USA

Website:	https://workbookpress.com/
Hotline:	1-888-818-4856
Email:	admin@workbookpress.com

Ordering Information:
Quantity sales. Special discounts are available on quantity purchases by corporations, associations, and others.
For details, contact the publisher at the address above.

Library of Congress Control Number:
ISBN-13:   978-1-952754-85-2 (Paperback Version)
                  978-1-952754-86-9 (Digital Version)

REV. DATE: 08/09/2020

Table of Contents

In her life, men taught her the different definitions of love.

Her father, the unhealthy, deviant type

Kenneth, casual sex

Saul, unconditional, parental love

Joseph, competitive love

Marcus, love for who she was

She grew into love and the hole in her heart was filled. Little girls should learn from

their first teacher, their father, a pure, healthy relationship.

PROLOGUE

Samantha is a young but amazing lawyer who rose through the ranks, thanks to the influence of her adoptive father, Saul. Saul and Samantha had their first encounter during a guest lecture at Georgetown, where Saul was to speak on the influence of politics in urban development. He had noticed Samantha in the second row, and something about her struck him. This intrigue translated into a blossoming relationship as Saul quickly discovered that she was a misfit in that town. Samantha was able to fit in with the elites because of her intellect. Instead of exposing her as someone who didn't possess the right to mingle with the high and mighty, Saul changed her story. He gave her a law clerk as a mother and became her father. With this new identity from struggling rogue to the daughter of a high society man, it was no surprise that doors began to open around, and she quickly rose through the ranks in her law firm due to her sheer determination.

Samantha's love life is another chapter of its own. Her foray into relationships started with a man who she had a fling with. However, it resulted in a pregnancy neither of them was ready to nurture. Feeling violated, she got rid of the pregnancy and moved on wounded. While in law school, she became close to a man named Joseph, who carefully drew her close to him until he revealed that he had always loved her. Already crazy in love as well, Samantha and Joseph started a whirlwind romance that was filled with hot sex and a passion that never dimmed. Although his parents never supported the relationship as they had other plans for him, Joseph continued to meet up with

Samantha as an act of defiance towards his parents. However, this romance ended in painful tears as he organized a getaway to give Samantha the worst news in her life.

Erroneously thinking that the getaway was only a prelude to a proposal from Joseph, Samantha was shocked when he announced to her that he had gotten another woman pregnant. Consumed by pain, she listened as he narrated how he slipped up with a lady who his parents had picked out from childhood as the one he would marry. He decided that he would have a low-key engagement with her to take care of the baby. Despite his insistence that it would only be a paper marriage, Samantha knew that their time together had come to a disastrous end.

Broken and dejected, Samantha was nursed back to life by her trusted assistant, Rick, and Marcus…the man who made her insides melt. Marcus was meant to be just a business client, but she couldn't resist the urge to penetrate through his calm exterior. Samantha seduced him after their meeting and spent a wild time between the sheets. Although she didn't know it early, her sheer dominance in bed and the control she exerted as she twisted his insides with pleasure had him hooked from the start.

There was something different about Marcus. Even though she still had strong feelings for Joseph, it was increasingly difficult to relegate Marcus to the back of her mind. It didn't help that he made a conscious effort to draw her closer. He showered her with attention until she couldn't deny it anymore and went into his arms. From there began another love story where the hot sex was never in short supply. It was a fantastic connection, and it would have gone well if things hadn't gone horribly wrong. Samantha never forgot about Joseph, and after a wild night in Marcus' arms, she couldn't resist the urge to call him again. Joseph wanted them to meet one more time, and she agreed. Marcus was making her feel uneasy, and all she wanted was to be with Joseph again. She would have gone through with it if she hadn't come down with severe flu symptoms that prompted her to visit the doctor. Shocked and distraught, she listened as she heard the dreaded sentence for the second time in her life…" you are pregnant." This puts her in a dilemma; WHAT HAPPENS NEXT?

Chapter 1

I could feel his rhythmic breathing next to me before I even opened my eyes. The heat of his naked body close by on the mattress brought each detail of the night before flooding back to my mind.

The tangible opulence of the restaurant with its glistening chandeliers…The pristinely dressed waiters bearing bubbling bottles of champagne- vessels of vice ready for the taking… The oriental rugs that muffled the sound of every footstep, as if drowning out the noise of those who walked in would keep their actions secret as well.

Perhaps others needed their dirty deeds kept secret, but not me. I was used to covering my tracks. I'd been doing it for a long time. By my estimation, my tactics had never failed. After all, I always ended up on top which was the ultimate goal.

I glanced over at Marcus. My body heated up over again as I watched him sleep. I remembered the ecstasy of digging my fingers into his rich, auburn curls, the sensation of his five o'clock shadow on the palm of my hand.

I carefully lifted my end of the covers, slipping out from beneath his arm which lay across my midsection. All I had to do was disappear from his luxurious apartment without waking him. Then my plan would be complete. It would be easy; I could tell he was out cold. I soundlessly gathered my things with practiced ease, tiptoeing into the bathroom to dress.

Samantha, you've done it again.

I'd certainly played him with this one. True, taking me

out to an extravagant restaurant, ordering wine, stressing his prominent position, had all been his idea, all a part of his grand plan. He thought all of the usual charms he pulled out to impress the ladies would wrap his new lawyer right around his finger. What he didn't know was that his lawyer knew that game backward and forward and never came out the loser. It was only a matter of time before he realized that he'd lost and I'd won.

Checkmate.

My phone began to buzz, reminding me that it was time for a new work week to begin before I even left Marcus's dwelling. I vacated the room, brand new pumps in hand. I moved far enough away from Marcus's door to ensure that he would not hear me before answering the phone.

"Hi, Rick." It was always Rick at this ungodly hour of the morning. "I have signed the contract and I've got a check for half a million right here in my hands," I said as I wriggled my feet into my shoes."

"Perfect."

Even from the other end of the line, I could tell that Rick was salivating over this victory.

Nothing could please him like half a million. Nothing except, perhaps, a full million.

"I knew you could pull this off, Samantha," he nearly purred. "Of course. Was there ever any doubt in your mind?" "None whatsoever."

I always got what Rick wanted. What we both wanted was to add Marcus and his distinguished father, a man who owned one of the wealthiest construction companies in New York, to my list of expensive clients. To men like them, my half-million-dollar retainer was just loose change.

"Go ahead and send out our welcome package to your lover boy's dad?" Rick suggested as I reached the elevator. "I'll schedule a reception for him early next week and invite all the contractor clients. It'll be a great way to show our new client the impressive names we have in our book."

I listened to Rick's ambitious chatter with only half of my attention. The other half was on the day ahead, the lists of things I had to do, the endless tasks at hand.

"I've got to run to the bank and deposit a check," I said cutting in. "Sorry I didn't take your call last night Rick, I got a little… tied up." A small smile spread across my lips. I knew full well that my choice of words would not be lost on Rick, but now he was in work mode. He'd want to know all about it later, once a few martinis did their job at piquing his curiosity.

"Can you make sure there's a change of clothes ready at the office for me? I'll have to take a shower there. I've barely slept and I could use one hell of a cup of coffee. Court's at eight and Judge Davis has been riding me all week."

Rick also helped me attend to the bidding of Saul Weinstein, my adopted father. Rick did him a huge favor by keeping an eye on me. I gave Saul a great deal back because of the position he'd helped me achieve. It was a small thing to offer considering all he had done. Without Saul, I would not be half of what I was today.

Once outside, I hailed a cab, giving directions to my law firm in Greenwich Village as I settled against the leather seat. Between playing my cards with Marcus and then an almost immediate phone call from Rick after waking up, this was the first time since the previous day that I was not working. As I watched the towering skyscrapers of Manhattan flypast, my thoughts drifted back to all that had happened after our deceptive little dinner…

I knew what he saw when he looked at me. A woman pretty, poised, and self-absorbed. But of course, that's what I wanted him to see- that's who I'd crafted Samantha to be. I wanted her to be an enigma, an uncrackable code, that made men want her more and more. I gave him little about myself and instead focused on him, learning every detail I could about the man who sat before me. Of course, I already knew most of it, I had a team of crack investigators that looked into every client I met with. It didn't hurt to have a little bargaining power in their background if needed. However, I would play the game, let Marcus think he was in control. He thought he was playing me. Another round of drinks came and went, and Samantha dug deeper, Marcus's lips loosened from the alcohol that flowed freely. The night wore on until the restaurant announced its closing. I was surprised to find myself reluctant to go. There was something about this man that I could not quite place my finger on. Reaching for my hand, Marcus held it tight in his, lips brushing over my bent knuckles. Electricity snaked through my body, and from the look on his face, he had felt it too.

"Seeing as you are much soberer than I am, and my apartment is not far from yours, would you be willing to drop me off?" A smile widened on his face, and I couldn't help but notice how his eyes dance when he smiled. I wasn't silly enough to believe that I was falling for him, but I felt like a cat watching a bird, ready to pounce. With one whispered word to the valet, his silver

Lamborghini glided around the corner, gleaming in the overhead lights. He stood close behind me as the valet opened the door, his hand on the small of my back, guiding me into the car. Music filled the car. There was no need for words. The car seemed to drive itself, slipping through the glistening lights of Manhattan. I said nothing as we missed the turn into my street.

Tall glass buildings towered ahead. Of course, Marcus lived in one of his father's most prestigious developments. The car glided to a stop and Marcus slid his keys over to the valet. I followed behind him wordlessly. The doorman punched the penthouse code into the elevator.

Another man opened the suite door the moment the elevator doors came apart. As quickly as help appeared, they disappeared, all without a single word being uttered.

Dim lighting flooded the apartment, floor to ceiling windows looked out over the city and towards Central Park. A gentle clink broke the silence as Marcus poured himself a scotch, neat. He took a sip and offered me the glass. I took it from him, determined not to let him see my hands shake, and held my face passive as the scotch glided down my throat. Oh, how I hated scotch, but I would not back down from a challenge with Marcus. I had to regain control of this situation, let him know who was in charge.

Throwing my black purse on the chair, I kicked off my heels, my stocking feet sunk into the carpet as I padded toward him, my mouth crashing down on his. I slid my tongue along his lips, they parted and I took him hungrily. His only choice was to give in to me. Every sense was already on fire. I slid my hand along the waist of his khakis, pulling his white shirt out and tearing it off his body. Underneath was pure perfection. His body was completely toned with a sculpted six-pack. My hands explored the hardness of his muscles, as I imagined him lifting weights and working day in and day out on construction sites. The soft light framed his face as his dark curly hair fell in his eyes. Those blue eyes pierced my very soul.

Next, my hands moved from his chest to cup his face as I kissed him ravenously. Marcus was the perfect mixture of two heritage's combined, his mother's European descent and his father's American ancestry. Now money, and lots of it, allowed him to take care of what God had given him. Meeting his gaze once more, I could see the surprise in his eyes. He had underestimated me, not seen me as the true woman that I was. He gave up any attempts at resistance and simply gave in to all my demands. I didn't bother to think about the hundreds of women that I was sure came before me, or the fact that I was not going to make him work for sex. Each move was purposeful, driven and I only had one goal in mind. Marcus would soon know who was truly in charge.

"Shall we move to the bedroom?" Marcus whispered in my ear as his lips traveled across my face and down my neck. He gave me no time to respond and instead held me close, maneuvering me toward his bedroom. Picking up my purse, I went with him willingly. Already the comfort, rather than the style of his apartment, shared that he did not bring many women back here. He preferred the ability to escape after a conquest. But I was not like every other woman.

My fingers expertly undid his belt and button, letting his khakis slide down his legs. With one firm pull, Marcus lay spread before me, my prey. I turned back towards the bedside table, silver glinting in my hands. I saw Marcus's eyes widen as he saw what they contained. I didn't even give him the chance to resist as the cold metal cuffed his wrists, the other end tying him firmly to the bed. I knew that he thought he had bought me, that the money was my motivator. My true desire was seeing that smug smile wiped from his face when he saw a woman in charge of her sexual desires.

I wondered how far he would let me go. A small smile played at the corner of my lips. It didn't escape Marcus, his blue eyes widened, his body strained towards me.

I could see the hardness of his cock, droplets gathering on its tip. The familiar ache between my legs called louder, it begged for a touch, a whisper. Rounding the bed once more, I pulled a small bottle from my purse and set it down on the nightstand. I could feel his eyes burning into me as my hands snaked around the back of my skirt and inched the zipper down slowly. Then it was at my feet. I gave him a cheeky smile before hooking my thumbs in my panties and sliding them delicately down my legs. Starting with his feet, my hands slid up his legs slowly, my hair teased as my body slowly followed. When my lips met his cock, I smiled at him and then guided his hardness into me. Marcus's body arched as low groans filled the air, his thrusts were urgent and full of desire. Leaning forward, I whispered in his ear.

"You are mine to do with as I please."

Pure pleasure shot through me as I saw his eyes grow larger and his expression bare within his very soul. He realized he had lost all control of the situation. He could do nothing but wait for my next move. My hips moved gently. This did nothing to relieve his swollen cock and he would not be encouraged to cum just yet. Leaning my body back, I cupped his balls in my hand momentarily before I slid my thumb inside of him. Confusion flashed across his face before pleasure once again replace it. His tense body told me that this was new to him, that nobody had teased him like this before. Reaching over him and retrieving the bottle from his nightstand, I undid the cap and gently poured its contents onto my stomach. The cool liquid flowed between my legs and over his cock. With slow, deliberate movements I wiped my hand across my smooth belly, the liquid in my hand. Lifting the object, I had tucked beside me, I dangled them suggestively in Marcus's face, letting his eyes widen as the realization hit. Running my hand up and down his balls, I let them become wet, with both our juices and the gel. The liquid burned like a fire within me, but it only intensified my ambition. Sliding the small chain of metal balls inside Marcus, I moved with his cock, harder and faster as my hands slid the balls in and out. I could feel his shaft twitch. He's finally ready, I thought to myself as I slid off him, my hands reaching for his manhood. It took seconds before he came, hard, long moans filling the room, my name on his lips. I sat and watched him, my hands resting on his belly as his eyes dropped, his breathing evening as sleep overcame him. I watched and waited to make sure he would not wake before I slid up his body and undid the handcuffs. A soft snore escaped his body as he rolled over, hands tight against his chest. Little did he know what had truly taken place.

"Here we are, ma'am."

The driver's words snapped me out of my reverie and I blinked, realizing for the first time I hadn't seen any of my surroundings on the familiar route to my workplace. All I saw in my daydreaming was him… Marcus… Fully at my mercy, calling out my name, his pleasure in my hands…

I disentangled myself from the memories, pulling money for the driver from my Louis Vuitton. I made my way to the front desk where the receptionist was ready with the change of clothes Rick had left for me. Twenty minutes later I was showered and walking through the halls of the office building, the usual activity of Monday morning buzzing around me. When I reached my office, I entered as if it were any other day. The fact that I'd been taking care of business well through the night was unnoticeable to anyone watching.

I had established a morning routine for such days like this, ensuring that I was able to get going without a hitch. Rick had it memorized just as well as I did. This kind of efficiency was necessary when it came to engaging with the high and mighty. Things worked differently in wealthy circles than they did on the ground level. Adjusting the deal-making strategy to include less orthodox methods was an occupational necessity and therefore treated with little ceremony. Rick knew the drill so I was not surprised, but still ever-so-grateful when I walked into my empty workspace to find a fully laid breakfast, every detail of my preferences attended to, the way only my assistant was capable of.

In truth, Rick was far more than my assistant. He was my paralegal, my confidant, and my friend. He knew how to comfort me and knew exactly what I needed. Sometimes he knew even before I did. From the first time I met him, it was like we had known each other in a past life. He knew my secrets before they passed my lips. He never judged, just simply helped me in any way he could. Occasionally, he would drive me home, fix me dinner, and tuck me in like I was his daughter. He was my closest and most trusted ally. In truth, I could not imagine trying to navigate the turbulent atmosphere I lived in without him.

He knew me better than anyone else on Earth, besides perhaps his husband Scott. The three of us had formed a kind of kinship. Their relationship was not something Rick spoke of frequently though he and Scott shared 20 years. They clearly cared for each other, but Scott found it necessary to conceal their bond, especially from his mother. She was a conservative woman and raised a son that reflected these values. Scott struggled against the difficulty of keeping his sexual orientation confidential. His careful attempts to hide this part of his identity were a stark contrast to Rick who flaunted his with pride.

The one place where Scott was able to find satisfaction was in supporting both himself and Rick. Though there was no need for him to work, Rick kept the job because he enjoyed it.

Scott was a retired stockbroker and years of owning his firm had left him without a care in the world and the ability to provide for his partner. Still, he too agreed that holding a job was a good thing. Rick was a social butterfly that thrived on interaction. He also possessed a particular buoyancy that was best put to use towards something constructive. If pent up, Rick's energy nearly drove Scott up the wall, fond as he was of him. Rick's job gave them both the perfect balance.

I worked my way through voice messages and emails as I ate, preparing myself both mentally and physically for the case I'd present with the hour. The first item on my list was Judge Ford. What a way to start the week. The man did little to disguise the fact that he was not particularly fond of me. There was something about me that was not his cup of tea which was fair enough- it wasn't as if I expected to be adored by everyone I met. However, this acceptance on my part did nothing to change the stilted nature of our interactions. Besides his distaste of me, Ford disapproved of the ways a number of my clients secured their Manhattan construction permits. This point of contention ensured that every conversation we had was permeated with an unmistakable level of repugnance. Today's case with my client Stirling Goddard was just the type that got under Ford's skin.

Never having been in the habit of letting the man's peccary nature mess with my mind, I finished my breakfast and mentally shifted gears. It was time for battle.

Chapter 2

By the time I stood before Judge Ford, I was the picture of professionalism. The change of clothes and revitalizing meal had done their work to disguise my activities from the previous night. I stood, ready to face my foe in front of a courtroom full of spectators.

Beside me sat Stirling Goddard, whose effort to obtain permits to build a highrise in the heart of the city would see the old train station building reduced to a pile of rubble. Goddard was a man of little sentiment. He failed to recognize the historical significance of the building. He saw it, instead, as prime real estate. Of course, how he had attempted to obtain the construction permits was less than legal and behind him, he had a trail of paid off inspectors who condemned the building. This certainly was not going to be a dull trial- never was in these matters.

"And what do you propose?" Ford asked, a frown settling across his face as he reached out for the case file in my hand. Crossing the courtroom floor, I handed the file over to Ford before speaking.

"My client has generously offered to repair the old station building, at his own significant personal cost, and register the building as a historical landmark. All we ask is to be allowed to incorporate the building into the plans of the highrise."

I didn't have to look at Goddard beside me to feel him blanch. He was less than happy with the idea, but he also knew that this was now our only option. On the other hand, Judge Ford was running for office and Goddard had made a rather generous campaign donation. I could see Ford's vein pulsing out of his forehead as he mulled the decision over.

He cleared his throat, "A member of the National Historic Associate will closely monitor all reconstruction and modifications. However, I cannot ignore the demands of the city's current housing crisis or the desires of my constituents and with that, I rule in the favor of Stirling Goddard's proposal."

The judge had no real option and his words were those of a man trying to save grace. Ford had already received a phone call from Saul who had reminded him that in his file, we had evidence of Ford's rather eclectic sexual preferences. Similar to the men that Ford liked to buy, he was just another bought judge in a long line that came before him. Saul had a file on everyone. He kept them locked away and only brought them out when someone needed a reminder of who was really in control.

Clapping my client on his shoulder, I handed him over the paperwork on the judge's orders and whispered some final words of advice. Goddard's eyes widened, but he said nothing as I slipped away from the table. Those wide eyes followed my ass as I walked across the courtroom and down the corridor.

I hadn't gotten halfway down the hallway before my phone began to buzz. I juggled my case notes in one hand while the other desperately searched through my bag. It was Saul. He always seemed to know just when everything started and ended for me. I expected his call since he would certainly want to hear that I'd been victorious.

"Hi, Saul. Judge Ford went for the proposal although I'm sure you know there was never any doubt. He accepted the slap on the wrist punishment and is still allowing Goddard to build around the station and incorporate it into the design."

"I have no idea what you are talking about my girl," Saul replied, though I could hear the smile lighting up his face.

"Sure..."

Saul laughed affectionately. He was well aware that I'd caught onto his ways over the years. He tried to remain elusive to many, but I knew he appreciated this aspect of our bond.

"I'm calling to see if you can still make it to the estate for dinner on Sunday?"

I could not recall making these plans. Still, even if I had forgotten and planned something else, it wasn't as if I would say no. There was nothing that trumped plans with Saul.

"Yes, we're on. Six o'clock?"

"You got it."

"Great, I'll see you then."

"One more thing," Saul said before I could hang up.

Once again, it was easy to read his mind. "We got the Matthew contract, a cool half million and they rolled over without a fight."

The smile reentered his voice. "There was never a doubt in my mind. You're one hell of a negotiator."

I grinned now too. "Thanks, Saul. See you Sunday."

His praise never failed to fulfill me in a way that nothing else could. This seemed natural enough considering Saul was my father. Our first encounter had been centered around his guest lecture at Georgetown on the influence of politics in urban development. He immediately sought me afterward at the reception, commenting that he could not help but notice me in the second row, the way I hung on his every word.

And he was right.

Saul's lecture had made something clear to me. At that moment I knew what I wanted to do with my life. I wanted to be Saul in the female form.

As it turned out, Saul was just as intrigued by me as I was by him. I was an enigma he couldn't quite figure out. Rather quickly, he discovered I was smart, extremely so, but that my over competitive streak was hiding something. He did not stop until he had uncovered my secret. It took him only a week to pin me down.

I discovered this when he laid before me a file about myself. The file revealed my spiraling debt and the ability to manipulate people to get what I wanted.

Saul knew I was an imposter.

Georgetown was a sea of senators' kids and I had only managed to fit in with the elites because of my intellect.

Had Saul decided to reveal to the authorities that I did not possess the "birthright" to be there, I would have been in huge trouble. The plans I had been clawing my way towards would be decimated. Yet, Saul did not do that. He had plans for me instead.

Rather than expose me, Saul created me. He took me from being a neglected child and made a new story for me. He assigned me a new mother, a law clerk who he was briefly involved with. She was generously compensated for going along with the tale Saul spun. Saul never told me this, I just knew.

The clerk agreed to say that I was her daughter and that after her brush with cancer and several years after her affair with Saul, she had decided to name him as my father.

Upon being handed this new identity, America's most elite circles opened up to me. It was not uncommon for me to spend my weekends skiing with the Kennedy's or

lunching with the Hiltons. In this world, nobody questioned my "father's" story. Saul's word was law. Brief affairs and secret love children were common among this breed anyways.

Once I had become more adapted to my role and my transformation from struggling rogue to high society daughter was complete, I spent the occasional Saturday on Saul's arm accompanying him to social events, donning the latest couture. There was nothing more important than power and money in Saul's world. With the help of his coaching and support, I fit right in.

All Saul ever asked for in return for the attention he paid to me over the years was my company on a Sunday night. Sundays were for dining in comfort and drinking brandy while playing chess. We would have wonderful debates about law. I would share my latest client challenges and we would strategize on the best way to win their cases.

He'd set me up well in this world. Whatever turn my life

took, no matter the situation, Saul was always there to make sure things worked out for me. If I asked him to, half an hour and a few quick phone calls were all it took to iron out any wrinkles in my path.

To turn my life around and ensure my success, he had taken complete control. He financed my law firm, oversaw the selection of staff, and even arranged my apartment across from Central Park. I wore only the latest clothes, and I had designer furniture in my office and apartment. Every few months, there was a new car. Saul had completely redesigned my life, giving me hope where previously I had none.

From the very start, Saul saw to it that my days were not all work and no play. I enjoyed months of luxury, months of traveling around Europe introduced to new cultures and sights that I had only ever dreamed of. Directly upon arriving back from over two months away, my life took another turn. It was then that I fell straight into the arms of Joseph.

Joseph, partnered with the other male figures in my life, was what shaped my feelings about men, my relationship to them, and my reactions toward them...the way it had shaped my reaction to Marcus...

My phone rang again. I looked down at it but stopped in my tracks when Joseph Claiborne's name lit up the screen. I had not heard from him in months, and yet, a familiar and overpowering ache still filled my body at the mere thought of him.

"Speak of the devil," I murmured as I lifted the phone to my ear. "Hello?" I could only hope that my voice sounded steady and in control.

"Sweetheart." The endearment left his mouth in a rush, sounding much like a breath of ecstasy, increasing the heat building between my legs.

Inside I chided myself for being so weak, but only half-heartedly. There was little point in trying to fool myself about the emotions Joseph stirred inside of me.

"It's great to hear your voice, why haven't I heard from you?"

"Hi, Joseph. My caseload has been beyond insane. The days just slipped by. I need to hire another paralegal to give me more time for the finer things in life." It did not take much for me to take on my usual tone with him...suggestive, teasing, sensual... I nearly purred the final phrase, knowing that my intimation would not be lost on him.

Joseph was like a drug, one drop of him and I wanted more. This explained the effect he had on a woman even as determined and independent as me.

We'd raced neck-in-neck with one another through law school. Joseph finished at the top of our class, putting me in a close second. That was when we truly met, the end of our schooling years when the rest of life was about to begin.

Our intellects matched perfectly. Due to the healthy level of competition between us, we made excellent sparring buddies, sharpening each other's thought processes and debate skills. All over the city, we could be found arguing over the latest court case or our motives as lawyers.

It was only a matter of time before we began to act on an intimate level as well. I began to experience the undeniable effect he had on me. Our chemistry was impossible to ignore.

Unfortunately, life tends to have a way of not working out quite the way one wishes.

Such was the case with Joseph and me.

"I'm coming to New York. I arrive tomorrow afternoon. Tell me you have a day off to show an old friend around."

It was not a question. It was a statement.

"I'll be there at 3, I'm flying in myself so no chance of delay. I need to see you."

I could envision him perfectly. He would be dressed in jeans and a linen shirt, no doubt wandering around his apartment in bare feet. No matter how much time we spent apart, it would have been impossible for me to lose the picture I had of him in my mind. Joseph's Adonis appearance was not an image that faded easily.

A beautiful man of mixed heritage, Joseph was well educated, and his physique was as fine-tuned as his brain. Everywhere he went woman admired him. When he was on my arm, I felt like the luckiest girl in the world. He was light-skinned with aristocratic features. Long loosely, curled hair, sculpted body. I could still recall what it was like to curl up against him or watch his arm muscles ripple as he carried me across the room to bed.

"Are you coming alone?" I hated to ask that question, but I also knew I could not face meeting one of Joseph's new women. We could have been good together if his parents had not interfered. They liked me, but they had plans for Joseph, plans that did not include me. Joseph, on the other hand, made it clear he was not ready to decide his future yet, personally or politically. Though he did not share his parents' opinions, he was too respectful to ignore them.

"Be there," he whispered into his phone. I could hear the lust in his voice. "It's been too long, my body needs you, I need you."

"I will be there Joseph," I said disconnecting our call. I did not ask him why he was coming to New York or where he would stay. He would be staying with me, in my bed, where he belonged.

I made my way towards my car. My mind was completely preoccupied with Joseph. The sound of his voice had brought so many memories and sensations flooding back. The conflict of interest with his parents left us in a strange place. Still, that never kept me from giving in to him. I probably always would.

Chapter 3

I punched in the code for the gate and drove my car to its appointed spot in the garage.

Two more secured entrances and I was in my apartment.

I wriggled my toes out of my shoes and padded across the soft grey carpet, grabbing a wine glass and a bottle of wine as I went. My last stop was the stereo where I switched on classical music. Settling down in front of the bay window, I poured myself a generous glass of my favorite red.

I looked out over the darkness of Central Park and let my mind wander through the events of the day. My brain still hadn't completely wrapped itself around the fact that I would see Joseph again in less than 24 hours. It had been nearly two years since our relationship had come to its tragic end and months since we'd spoken. During the time after our break-up, I often felt sure that a passionate experience like ours couldn't possibly be finished off that easily. At other times, I was convinced I would never hear from him again.

Truthfully, something inside me had never fully been able to accept that. Somehow, I knew that he would find his way back to me.

When my phone buzzed to life, vibrating frantically on the table next to me, it caused me to jolt. I had been deeply caught up in my musings. Thankfully, my wine glass was nearly empty or I would have ruined my cream suit.

I exhaled, inwardly. Once again, the moment I thought I was

getting some time for myself I was proven wrong. At times like this, the demands upon me felt endless with someone always wanting something. Between my job and now Joseph and Saul...

That was slightly unfair. When I saw Saul's name on the caller ID, as always, I felt no resentment at all.

I might be in a tired fog of a long day, but nothing would stop me from answering him. "Hi, Saul I haven't forgotten about dinner on Sunday. I promise," I said turning away

from the window.

Saul's laugh rang from the other end. "I'm glad you haven't forgotten. I would hate to be stood up."

I shook my head, wryly. He knew as well as I that I would never stand him up. "Even if I did, it would take all of ten minutes for you to find a replacement. A million women are tripping over themselves to spend a night with Saul Wallenstein. Did you want me to bring anything over when I come for dinner?"

"I was wondering if you would care to spend the night. I wanted to know if Rosa should pick up some of that muesli you seem to like so much." I could almost hear Saul's nose wrinkle in disgust. He was a simple man and didn't believe in any of this new superfood business. I, on the other hand, loved to take care of my body.

"I'll spend the night if you promise to share some of that old cognac with me, you know the one you keep hidden behind the bookcase."

Saul's tone was amused. "You drive a hard bargain, Samantha.

Always have."

"Well, a girl has to have some talents," I teased.

"I rang to find out if you had a date for the charity ball on Saturday?"

"A date? Aren't I going with you, Saul?" I couldn't remember the last time he'd told me to bring a date. We'd always gone together.

"I want you to invite Marcus Matthews"

A spark of shock jolted through me and I half-wondered if Saul had been able to read my earlier thoughts. God knew, he was capable of almost anything.

The very idea of bringing Marcus along as if he were some ordinary date had my heart in my throat, blocking all but enough air to keep me from suffocating completely.

My actions of the prior evening went against every moral line I had established. I had never seduced a client before, but Marcus was too cocky, too sure of himself. Subduing him had felt like the only way. It was necessary.

What scared me most wasn't that I'd taken a creative route with my new client. It was that there was a sexual tension between us that was undeniable. I was sure that he would be awake by now, feeling a little bruised and tender. Did he remember what I had done, or had sleep and lots of wine reduced me to only the ghost of a memory?

I didn't want to find out. At least not like this. My mind begged Saul not to make me do it, but I knew that no matter what the cost I would never voice them out loud. I couldn't.

I did my best to compose myself and was pleased with how calm my voice sounded when I did speak. "Don't you think a business relationship is enough connection with that bunch?" Acting like I hadn't just slept with Marcus was no use, but I figured it was worth a shot.

"Why not?" Saul responded, smoothly.

I shook my head. Yes, why not?

"Sure, I can do that." It was my standard reply when it came to Saul. He knew that would be my answer, asking was just a formality.

"Fantastic," Saul said. The smile was back in his voice. "You'll make a fine pair."

I massaged my temples with two fingers of my free hand as I thought back on our night together.

Uh-huh, we sure do.

"So, I'll see you there?" I said, more than ready to be alone with my thoughts. "Yes, see you there. Get some rest. You've worked hard today."

"Amen to that," I muttered after hanging up.

The message Saul delivered by telling me to bring Marcus was clear.

Joseph ran his own environmental law firm, received monthly installments from a trust fund his grandfather had set him up, and he had been filthy rich since birth. Apart from the inherited wealth (I'd had to earn mine), Joseph and I were cut from the same fabric. Though we landed in the same social bracket, Saul believed him to be far from suitable for me.

Damn, it was like he'd been listening in on the conversation I'd just concluded with Joseph.

No, he hadn't been listening in. Once again, he just knew.

Saul didn't believe Joseph was good enough for me. No one ever had. From the start, the reasons had been black and white. Literally.

I'd been under the impression that in modern times racial prejudice had decreased significantly due to natural development. I was proven sorely wrong. When Joseph's parents saw their presidential son had fallen for a white girl, they made their position clear, an interracial relationship would never work.

Joseph lived a privileged life and wanted for nothing materially, academically, or sexually. He could have any of the many women who set their sights on him...beautiful and (mostly) intelligent women, but instead, he was satisfied with me.

I wasn't ugly by any means. Short, petite with graceful features. I had curly auburn hair that fell to my waist, unruly in every inch. My best feature was my eyes. Sea blue and wide, they were framed with long lashes. My eyes were quite effective at communicating my feelings, whether it was a wide-eyed look of surprise or a heavy-lidded look of desire. I understood the art of seducing a man with my eyes alone. A little body language never hurts either.

Joseph had softened me about six months into our relationship. Although he had always been kind and thoughtful, and we enjoyed each other's intellect, Joseph and I were strictly friends. I was attracted to him, but I made no moves and neither did he. We didn't talk about sex or anything related to it. Still, he was affectionate. There were plenty of innocent hugs and occasional teasings when he beat me on tests.

As our attraction to each other continued to grow, I got the sense that he wanted things to go farther. And frankly, so did I. Joseph and I continued to pursue one another, playfully, intellectually, and finally, sexually. I vividly remembered the forbidden camping trip on which our consummation had taken place.

We had a long weekend at school and Joseph had suggested a nice, secluded trek, just the two of us.

"What will your parents think?" I'd asked.

Joseph flashed me a confident smile. Suddenly, nothing and no one else in the world mattered. "Who said we were going to tell my parents? They don't have to know everything we do."

It was on this trip that he made his fatal move toward me. He pulled me into him forcefully. His chest was warm and I could hear his heart beating. We had just finished setting up camp and when I rolled out my sleeping bag he made his move.

The air had grown crisp, and the heat from his body was comforting. He smelled like cologne and smoke from the fire. I fit perfectly in his arms. We had planned this trip to be the last one before winter.

I never thought he would want to cross the line from friend to lover. He stroked my tangled hair. Joseph loved my hair down and was always teasing me about it being a mess. He bent down and nuzzled my neck. He whispered that I smelled good then took his hand and lifted my chin so he could see my face. With great passion, he kissed me fiercely on the lips. From that kiss, I was branded forever his.

I was rigid at first but very quickly I melted into his body, putting my arms around his neck and reaching to tug his curly hair as we continued a sensual kiss. His tongue explored my mouth. I relaxed for the first time in years and gave myself to him. I could trust Joseph with my feelings, something that was very new to me. I had grown to like Joseph. It was turning into love, maybe, but I had always kept myself distant from him.

Joseph did not speak, but I could feel his warm breath on my head as he held me to him. I tried to pull away. I desperately didn't want to ruin this friendship, and I knew that sex would change us.

Yet, there was an undeniable electricity, and he pulled me back and then bent to kiss me. He devoured my lips. At first, I wouldn't return the kiss, but as he pressed harder I finally relented and allowed passion to take over. I kissed him back, sucking the air out of him. He was tearing through my wall, and I was letting him in.

He stepped back and looked into my glazed eyes. Softly he said, "Sweetheart, I want you and you are safe with me. Do you want me?"

I pulled his head close to mine and kissed him hard. He picked me up in response and continuing our kiss, he laid me on the sleeping bag next to the fire. There, he stopped long enough to stroke my hair back away from my face. He was waiting patiently for me to accept his advances. His eyes were darker than usual, a mixture of lust and something I couldn't quite understand.

It was clear he wanted me, but only if I was comfortable with it. This was new to me, this feeling that I had toward him. Normally, I would move immediately to sex and then be finished with my conquest. This was not the case with Joseph.

I felt shy with him like it was my first time. A virginal feeling washed over me. I pulled him close. I wanted him and fervor burned deep inside of me. I could no longer contain it, I needed him and now I could have all of him. He kissed me gently, three pecks in a row, and then pressed his lips hard on mine, opening my mouth to receive his tongue. Simultaneously, he reached under my denim shirt and rubbed my back. His touch was tantalizing, and I forced my breasts toward him. My nipples were hard and I wanted them free of all clothing. I felt like I was burning. I was hot with desire for him.

He sat back and removed his coat and shirt. We were both wearing insulated underwear. Longingly, I gazed at his perfectly sculpted chest. He then began to unbutton my shirt, very slowly, it felt like he was purposely torturing me. He reached down the bottom of my tee-shirt, and instinctively I held my arms up as he pulled the shirt up over my head. My hair was now a tangled mess. I wanted him to touch my breast, and then release them into his hands. He instead pulled my head back using a hand full of my hair and kissed me fully on the lips. Then he planted kisses down my neck until he reached the edge of my bra, stopping there and supporting himself on his elbow. He whispered softly, "Tell me what you want."

"I want you!" It felt like I was screaming despite my barely audible voice.

He nuzzled my neck and began chewing ever so gently on my ear. I could not stand my pent up longing, "Joseph fuck me now, hard", I demanded. He smothered my words with a deep throat kiss. He reached down and pulled his erection out of his long johns. It was hard and ready. He pulled down my underwear, took his hands, and spread my legs apart. He separated the lips of my vagina by rubbing his cock back and forth. I was wet and ready for him. He thrust himself into my pussy. The pure force of his thrust had me gasping for air. Slowly, he began to move his body up and down.

I moved my body to match his rhythm. We were moving together as one body, I felt the building of my desire. Gasping, I softly moaned, "Fuck me harder." He obeyed and increased his weight on me. My body responded by bursting into orgasm. Joseph sensing that I was ready, released his climax. He had amazing control, he was not selfish in his lovemaking. He waited until we came together.

Joseph was not finished with me. He released my bra and sucked on my nipples, teasing them with gentle nips of his teeth. Joseph began rolling them between his fingers while kissing my stomach until he reached my vagina, he seemed to like that I kept my pubic hair shaved. From there, he licked my clitoris until I could no longer stand the pleasure. My arousal began to peak again. Joseph moved his body so he could thrust his hardness once more. I came with the first thrust, and he collapsed on top of me.

Exhausted from the sex, the climb, and the excitement that Joseph had finally committed to me, I fell asleep. He covered me with the sleeping bag and kissed me gently.

"I love you and you are safe with me".

He then got up and put logs on the fire, I could see his naked body from the firelight. He walked down to the lake and jumped in the water. It must have been cold, But Joseph was the type of man that could endure a little discomfort.

When he returned to the sleeping bag, he zipped us both in. His naked body was entwined around mine. His body heat helped me drift. My mind was clear and I was content, falling into a deep sleep.

When I awakened, the sun was starting to rise. It was beautiful and I wanted to share it with Joseph. His muscular arms were wrapped around me as he slept soundly. I didn't want to wake him, but the fire had died down and I was getting cold.

He smiled at me as he blinked his eyes open. He nuzzled my hair and kissed my neck. His stubble scratched my skin but I didn't mind. He was so boyish like this. He seemed playful.

"You're probably cold. I'll warm you up." He kissed me deeply. Between my legs, I ached in anticipation. My breasts felt his lips, once again he nipped them playfully. The pain and the pleasure intensified my increasing moisture. He teased my nipples with his fingers. I drew closer to him. Taking charge, I mounted him. My desire was consuming me and I wanted him now. He chose to take his time, although the fire was out and I was naked.

The air was crisp, a true fall morning. I shivered and felt goosebumps form along my body.

Somehow the cold made every feeling more intense. I straddled him, his hard cock pressing up against me.

Joseph's arms folded under his head as he leaned back with a grin. He had no intention of controlling me and simply laid back to watch the show.

My tangled hair fell forward covering my face as I reached under his ass and maneuvered his penis against the lips of my vagina. The weight of my body caused me to take all of him in one hard thrust. I was so wet that there was no reason for foreplay.

With sudden urgency, he pushed my hair back and flipped me over on my back. Our bodies never disconnected. His eyes were a deep shade of brown, signaling the intensity of his desire. From our new position, he took charge and began to thrust his body bringing me to the height of pleasure. Then, just as I was about to climax, he slowed his pace. He was now in control and I was the one begging.

Joseph began to move slowly, entering me gently until I was there again, fully ready to explode my passion on to him. Joseph knew he was commanding my body to meet his rhythm. Once we moved together, he began to thrust faster. I met his rhythm again and wrapped my legs around his torso, bringing us even closer. His naked body was pulled deeper inside of me.

We climaxed together as I cried out, "Fuck me harder!"

He kissed me hard to smother the words that came out of my mouth. I always cursed when I climaxed, something Joseph disapproved of. He rolled me onto my stomach, I knew what was coming next. Forcefully, he slid his arm under my waist to lift me to my knees, spread my legs apart, and rammed his cock into me from the back. Joseph moved so quickly that I didn't have time to recover from the first orgasm.

"I will fuck you, but that is the end of the profanity. You will be punished each time you use those words."

He kissed my back and thrust hard until he collapsed beside me on the sleeping bag. He knew that I had not climaxed the second time. His lovemaking had been rough. Luckily, the sun was rising and bringing its warmth to the day.

"Sweetheart, are you hungry? Are you ready to eat?"

I remembered so clearly our washing in the lake together. Joseph dove right into the lake. I preferred to sit on the bankside only sticking a toe in because the water was so cold. I could still hear his laughter and all the new things he taught me about nature, life, pleasure, and love. Even the delicious smell and taste of his campfire pancakes with fresh maple syrup lingered.

"Should we talk about this?" I asked. I was so uncertain of what this was.

Joseph looked me in the eyes as if he was peering into my soul. "I wanted you from the first time I met you. It didn't seem like you trust people easily, so I was patient. I waited for you to get to know me first."

"Joseph that was two and a half years ago. You never made a single move toward me. Such amazing restraint you have," I mused.

"I knew what I wanted, Samantha. I also knew it was going to be complicated, but not just on your end. You should know what you are getting into with my family. They have certain expectations of me. I'm not sure yet if I share them." I was aware of Joseph's background, but I am not sure either of us realized the influence it would have on our future.

At the campsite, it was only the two of us. While still cocooned in ignorant bliss Joseph declared, "Sweetheart, you make me happy. I feel like I have found my friend, my lover, and yes my soulmate. Let's see where we go. I love you, Samantha.

That was four and a half years ago and now he was returning to my life. I could only hope Joseph had finally decided what he wanted. Back then, he promised we would be together. Now I was ready.

After we returned from the camping trip, Joseph had already moved my stuff into his apartment. He never asked, he just assumed. I didn't question his actions, it was what I wished for. I wanted whatever Joseph wanted. Unfortunately, Joseph did not always know what that was.

I never discovered if Joseph's parents found out about our camping trip. Even if they had no notion of what their son did, Saul, of course, seemed to know my every move. He didn't scold me, he rarely did. Even after Joseph and I moved in together for a brief, erotic time, Saul never said he disapproved in so many words, but he somehow always made his stance known with the quiet control that was so much a part of him.

There were times when I completely understood that it would be better for everyone if I broke things off with Joseph. Those times had grown more frequent lately. This warranted more wine, so I filled my glass to the top.

I knew that I wasn't going to break things off. Not now. Maybe not ever. The promise Joseph had made to me was still firmly cemented within my consciousness. "One day we'll be together" he'd said. "Because you know that there's no one who can satisfy you like me, baby."

I looked down at my wine glass in puzzlement, hardly able to believe how quickly I'd downed my second glass.

Joseph had been the one to break me in. He taught me the feeling of giving and receiving love in all its passion. He'd understood my need for reassurance. Through his promises that he was mine to do with as I pleased, he'd stoked the embers within me. Dreams awakened within me that the protection he pledged to me might continue long after graduation.

For a time, I believed this might come to fruition. Life was good for us. We made love frequently, in between classes and throughout the night which made life daring, exciting.

Joseph would have dinner with Saul and me every Sunday. It was impossible not to enjoy their intelligent probing of each other's minds. Joseph's parents liked me and his grandfather adored me as well. I tried my best to ignore the fact that I did not fit into their plans for their son.

Saul sought to protect me from harm whenever possible. He attempted to direct me towards others.

By replacing Joseph he hoped to avoid heartbreak.

In spite of his subtle prodding, I knew that Saul sympathized with me. He'd told me of his long-standing relationship with an alluring black woman. He remained faithful to her for many years while she tended to his house and saw to his more intimate needs. I remembered his face when he told me, the spark in his eye, the softness that appeared around his face.

No one spoke of it. The reality of the relationship remained so

Patricia Boyer-Weisman

hushed that at times I questioned whether it was true. However, remembering Saul's gentleness in coping with my attraction to Joseph assured me the stories were honest. He understood my inextricable bond to Joseph and the feelings that bonded me to him. I stayed because I knew no one could take control of him the way I could. The battle between us felt eternal. This was not a sensation I intended to part with anytime soon.

I made my way down to my office and unlocked the door with practiced ease all while checking emails on my phone. I was so engrossed in getting started with my day that the man in my office went unnoticed.

"Fancy seeing you here."

I jumped, my eyes shot up from my email, and a disconcerted frown formed across my face. My annoyance quickly transformed to surprise when I realized Marcus was standing before me.

"I thought that when a person's secretary left you a message to call, that's what you did. Showing up at my doorstep is a little dated, don't you think?"

"I'm hardly on your doorstep. Arriving at your house wouldn't be appropriate, would it?"

His implications were not lost on me, but I opted to ignore the bate. "Well, I guess, my office is fine."

Though Marcus was put together, I could see that the effects of the previous night's activities had not fully worn off. I certainly must have made an impression considering he dared to show up in my office after he'd been as good as beaten during our last encounter.

43

There was a tenderness to him that could not be hidden. Every gesture and word sent a surge of satisfaction through me. I felt bold enough to press on to fulfill Saul's request.

"Since you are here, I might as well tell you now," I said, making my way around my desk to set my things down. I picked up the cup of steaming hot coffee Rick had left me and took a long sip. When the silence lengthened and I continued to drink, Marcus's brows rose in curiosity.

"Do tell."

I studied him for a moment, averting my eyes from his unwavering gaze. I hated the power his mere presence had over me. It reduced me to a shy schoolgirl and I could hardly believe what I'd done to this fine specimen a few hours prior.

"You are cordially invited to join Saul and me at a charity ball on Saturday."

Marcus's eyes flashed, taken aback. "Is this the way you usually treat clients after a night like ours?"

So I hadn't been reduced to a ghost in his mind.

I snorted, answering before I could think it through. "It's not as if I have many nights like ours." Now it was Marcus's turn to appear satisfied and I cursed myself inwardly. I must not let my guard down or make him feel that he had control over me. At least not too much.

"So? Are you in?" I asked, attempting to divert his attention.

Marcus studied me for a moment before smiling with his

eyes. His chin tilted up in defiance. "You bet I'm in."

"Good."

I fiddled with the things on my desk, still feeling flustered at his sudden appearance. Stumbling in with an armload of work and immediately gulping down my coffee wasn't how I'd pictured the second interaction playing out. He had gall showing up bright and early on a weekday when my message had specifically told him to call. For him, being absent for one day of work every once in a while, with no notice was a non-issue. Guaranteed inheritance of his father's construction business, a hefty trust fund from his grandfather, and a secure place on the staff as a crane operator likely afforded him many passes.

I jerked myself back to the present when I realized I'd been studying his lips for far too long. I hoped he hadn't noticed, but when our eyes met, I knew I'd been caught and Marcus was doing his best to take full advantage of it.

A grin stretched across that tantalizing mouth as he sat down in the chair across from my desk. He was a ladies' man, that was for sure. Truthfully, he was a people's man to be more accurate. I was determined not to let his smooth, deliberate way of talking, get to me. I intended to always be on top in all capacities.

I found it amusing that he chose to sit while I stood, placing himself in a place of vulnerability, similar to the previous night. I hated to admit that I wanted more than anything to have my way with him in this manner once more.

"Would you do something for me?" I asked when he continued to simply watch me. He seemed to expect us to shut the blinds and go for it right there on the floor as if I had nothing better to do.

"I would like to think I can," Marcus responded.

"Could you get out so I can get some work done?"

He let out an amused chuckle as he stood. "Sure. I should be getting back anyway." "Ah, so you do have a job," I said, my tone clipped. "I was starting to wonder."

Marcus grinned. "I was talking about my motorcycle. I don't like leaving it exposed out in the open for long. I prefer seclusion for its safekeeping."

He left me alone then, shaking my head at his final innuendo.

One thing was for certain, Saturday night was going to be something.

Chapter 4

I pulled into the airport's cell phone area to kill a few minutes while I waited for Joseph's plane to land. The plane was a gift from his grandfather. Joseph loved his toys, both animate and inanimate. Unlike most spoiled rich kids, Joseph did not have everything handed to him.

Joseph was expected to know how to take care of himself. He could change the oil and tires. He knew about engines. He packed his parachute for skydiving, swam with great skill, and performed CPR. He was educated in household tasks as well. Whether he was running the washing machine or operating a sewing kit, Joseph was capable. Additionally, he spoke three languages and volunteered each summer in a third world country as a teenager.

Though he was to inherit his grandfather's fortune, he'd been taught how to manage money from a young age. His grandfather had seen to it that he received both a practical and academic education, sculpting his humanitarian view and focus on the bigger picture in life. Such knowledge came with even greater accountability. His family never failed to reinforce this.

The fact that his parents pushed him to excel in everything he did put an unreasonable amount of pressure on his shoulders and drove him to work twice as hard as anyone else. I'd seen him snap under pressure before. When living up to their every expectation became too much, he rebelled, taking off on his own, indulging in the activities that halted progression toward their ultimate plan for him.

This was likely what this pitstop to see me was about. It was one of those times when life's circumstances had spurred him to revolt, sending him directly into the arms of his greatest vice. After working out his inner struggle with the demands of his parents he would return back to his ceaseless striving according to their wishes. For now, I was what he needed. He was mine.

Ordinarily, I would have used the spare chunk of time to answer emails and make quick phone calls, but I found myself unable to focus on either. I eventually set my phone aside and turned my gaze to the runway as I allowed my mind to dwell on Joseph.

Due to his arresting physique and his commanding presence, Joseph was guaranteed to get what he wanted in life and bed. He was an impossible man to forget. The combination of distance and a demanding work schedule had managed to displace him from my head for a short time. Now that he was only minutes away from me, I wondered how that had been possible.

He had redefined my experience with men, crafted my view of myself in so many ways, that I knew that he'd be an integral part of me for the rest of my life. Before Joseph, my education in men was vastly different. I leaned back in my seat, half wishing that I had the presence of mind to work instead of reminiscing in the memory of one of the first lessons I learned. Suddenly, as it often did, my mind slipped to the far away nightmares of Kenneth. The man who taught me my second lesson in love. A contribution to my destructive ways with the heart.

I met Kenneth at a bar when I was visiting my brother, Paul. When Kenneth walked into the bar, he drew the attention of all the women there, including myself. He was rugged, good looking and physically fit. His dark hair needed a cut but matched the rough exterior of who he was. Paul called him over and introduced us. They had gone to school together. Kenneth and I were immediately attracted to each other. He asked Paul who owned the white convertible in the parking lot. The bar didn't normally have the type of clientele that drove sports cars. The car was mine, of course, it was a white convertible that I'd worked hard to pay off.

The story was pretty par for the course. Kenneth wanted me and he quickly made it known. He even asked Paul if he minded if I drove him to his house. My brother gave his blessing. He was busy with a busty blonde anyways.

I played the game of being a helpless female. I thought I could control Kenneth, but I was too young and inexperienced in the game. I still hadn't learned that a hard dick has no conscience. I was just another notch in Kenneth's belt. He was used to the local girls. The cats that wore too much makeup and were comfortable being screwed over until they eventually landed their meal ticket. I was a different piece of ass, more polished, educated. He liked that air of sophistication. Though I didn't fully recognize it, he had every intention of having his complete way with me. And he did, by God, he did.

My mind instinctively pulled back from what happened next. For a time, I had drawn a blank, but nowadays, the memory came back with stinging clarity. There was never a good time for those memories. They hardened me. I promised myself that I would never be overtaken in that manner again. Then there was Joseph...

The door to my reverie slammed abruptly shut when my cell phone buzzed. It was him.

Here.

I exhaled, grateful to be forcefully removed from my thoughts as I started the car. My eyes searched for a glimpse of Joseph. I squinted at the cockpit but saw no trace of him. I smoothed my hands down the form-fitting dress I'd chosen. The feel of my firm thighs and slim waist gave me confidence. I'd tamed my curly mass of hair and put on a little extra lipstick as well.

I told myself that there was no reason to make a fuss, it was Joseph. Still, the very sight of him when he finally stepped out of the plane sent shivers and heat through my body at the same time.

He was beautiful. His hair was longer, and it suited him. He had on a leather bomber jacket and looked like an ad for a man's cologne, rugged yet polished to perfection.

The moment his eyes locked with mine, I could sense his need for me and I ceased to restrain myself. He had to descend the stairs from the plane two at a time, grabbing onto me with ravenous desire the moment I reached his arms. His embrace felt desperate as he locked me into his musky smell. I allowed myself to melt fully into his arms, greedily accepting his hungry kisses.

Swiftly, he unclipped the clasp that had been holding my unruly curls in place. He loved my hair a mess. He pushed me back and looked at the woman before him. His gaze devoured every detail of my face as if he couldn't take in the sight of it fast enough. When he did speak, his voice was husky with thirst.

"God, I have missed you. Are you ready to go? I have my plane ready to take you to dinner. I do not want to waste any time getting you out of that dress." He kissed me again and I allowed him to help me walk up the stairs to his plane. That was Joseph. Nothing he did was ordinary.

Barry, who had worked with Joseph's family for years and served as co-pilot of the plane, nodded respectfully to me. He'd always been a professional, mild sort of man who wordlessly communicated that he knew I was special to Joseph. I was the only one he ever invited on to his private jet.

Initially, his presence on the plane while Joseph and I fornicated in the bedroom had embarrassed me. That was no longer the case. Especially now when we were so ready to catch up. The whole world could have been outside our door and I could have cared less.

"Do I dare ask where we are going?" I questioned, forcing myself to form cognitive words.

Even as his eyes continued to study me with unabashed lust.

Joseph laughed. "Well, I was thinking somewhere warm. How about we go to the Boca house until Saturday? I called Rick and he said he could handle things at your office. I'm sorry if I screwed your schedule up. I just wanted it to be a surprise. Can you spare the time?"

"You know I won't say no. Can I assume you've taken care of everything?"

"Of course my darling. Marge has a glass of champagne waiting for you as we speak." Marge was a very attractive hostess that Joseph's family employed when they traveled. She had been around as long as Barry. I did not know her as well, but she was always friendly and it was nice having another woman on board.

Marge appeared immediately, handing me a glass of champagne in a monogrammed crystal champagne glass. There was a strawberry floating in the bubbles of the champagne. She also set a cheese and fruit tray on the table next to my chair. I listened while Joseph went over the flight checklist for the plane's departure. I never worried about Joseph flying the plane. He was always thorough and in control.

Today, he had something on his mind, I could see it in his eyes. I pushed any concerns away and focused on my increasing anticipation. I ached to feel his lips on mine and his hard penis inside of me.

I sat back, watching as he saw to every detail that could warrant his attention so that he could turn his full focus on me.

"Sir, your mother left a message for you while you were out," Marge said as Joseph's eyes moved over the flight plan. "She wanted to let you know that she and your father have landed safely in Bethesda and would like for you to call them at your earliest convenience."

The primly worded note did nothing to disguise the fact that nothing Joseph's mother requested was left to his convenience.

"Okay, I'll call her when I get back," Joseph responded, his attention remaining on the flight plan. "She says that the weather there this time of year is doing your grandfather good," Marge continued. Joseph was by far his grandfather's favorite amongst his grandchildren and Joseph's arresting face visibly softened at the mention of him.

The gentleness on his face arose just as much fervor in me as one of passion, making my hands itch to reach for him. However, I knew he was focused and settled on speaking to him instead.

"Are your parents visiting your grandfather then?"

Joseph shook his head, his eyes going back to the flight checklist. "They're in Bethesda to stay. They're retiring near Grandfather since his health has worsened and he needs more care."

I knew that since his wife's passing, Joseph's grandfather had never been the same. This was true for the entire family.

When Joseph spoke of his grandmother, he painted a picture of grace, and decorum. She was the type who lit up a room with her French elegance simply by entering. She took Joseph everywhere with her since his parents were away a large portion of the time. Under her guidance, he was groomed in the way of her social graces and passion for humanitarian issues. She'd adored Joseph just as his grandfather still did and there was no missing the impact she made on his life. Joseph was 17 when she passed after a battle with cancer, but a shadow still crossed over his face at the mention of her. She'd been more of a mother to him than his real one, making the wound of her passing an impossible one to heal.

Joseph's eyes remained on the checklist, but I knew from the lines along his brow and the hard set of his jaw that his thoughts were with his grandparents. As I watched him wrestle with his thoughts, trying his best to conceal them, thoughts of a completely different nature coursed through my mind. Heat shot through my body. I wished to take him to bed so that I could wipe away that pain on his face, making him forget it all. He would forget everything but me.

"About ready?" I asked, crossing my legs in an attempt to keep my burning craving for him at bay a bit longer.

A slight smile came to Joseph's mouth as he glanced over

at me. "Yep." He handed the checklist back to Barry before directing his attention my way. He possessed a glint in his eyes in spite of the residual sadness that still lined his lips, the lips I was impatient to feel on my skin.

He drew near, picking up his champagne glass and taking a seat across from me, teasing me with the leisurely nature of his every movement, fully aware I was being consumed with desire. Foreplay wasn't his forte. He preferred to work me up before he touched me, casting his spells with his mere presence. There lay a clear promise in his gaze of what was to come. Once we got down to business, he went in with full force. As always, I would be ready.

I remained patient as we talked for another hour, allowing my insides to prepare for the pleasure ahead, measuring his calm stride for stride.

By the time we'd finished with the 'pleasantries,' the sexual tension between us had become tangible. When Joseph finished his glass of champagne and stood, I knew it was time.

Joseph reach for my hand, "Shall we? 'he asked. He unfastened his belt and then mine. With ease, he pulled me out of my chair and led me to the bedroom.

I loved him and was grateful for whatever time we had together. He sat on the bed beside me and I took his hand and kissed the back of it, it smelled of soap. I placed his finger in my mouth and sucked on it, moving from finger to finger. Joseph's eyes were a dark brown that signaled intense emotional feelings. He took me on his lap and kissed me engulfing my mouth with his. Then he laid me down on his bed. His passion could not be measured, it was so intense. There was a new feeling of urgency about him, he began to unbutton my dress very quickly and without fully undressing he pulled his cock from his pants and slipped it into my panties parting my legs with his legs. Joseph plunged into me and I moaned as he entered. All thoughts now left my brain as he rode me until we both burst into ecstasy. After we reached our peak, he took his clothes off and undressed me and he began a tender exploration of my body. He caressed my breast and rubbed his penis across my stomach. He kissed me long and with great force. It was as if he was trying to suck my being into his. He kissed my neck and moved down to my stomach. He cupped his hands under my butt and lifted me to receive him. Joseph was different, he was tender, over and over he said, "I love you. I will always love you, no matter what. Wait for me my darling."

It was getting time for us to get dressed for landing, we were about an hour from Boca. Joseph pulled me to my feet, my hair was tangled and loose around my back. He held me against him for a moment then breathed into my hair. I knew there was something he wanted to say. Joseph could not be rushed, He would tell me when he was ready.

We stepped into the plane's intimate shower. Joseph lathered a washcloth and slid it between my legs. He gently rubbed my pussy, stimulating my clitoris. I leaned back into him, our naked bodies pushed together. He moved to clean me from behind, being careful to wash my anus. He rinsed out the washcloth and lathered it again. I held my arms up for him to wash under my breasts. He grabbed my hands and turned my body to him. His cock was hard and ready. I lathered a fresh washcloth and carefully rubbed his pulsing erection. The mere friction of the cloth made his penis harder. He had fire in his eyes. Suddenly, he pinned my arms above my head and rammed his penis inside of me. The water cascaded down on our naked bodies. We peaked rapidly. He kissed me passionately. The water was beginning to get cold as it trickled over our heads. We exited the shower and dried off with warm, fluffy towels.

The crew knew better than to disturb us. The only signal we received came from the speaker, announcing the plane's descent.

"Ready to go? I need to land," he said, removing the towel from his waist and tossing it over his shoulder.

I let my eyes roam his body one last time before nodding.

"Are you hungry?" he asked as he grabbed jeans and a linen shirt from the dresser. "Famished," I responded, retreating to the dressing table that was all prepared for me. "Good, we'll go to Georgina's."

It was well past 8 PM, but Chef Georgina was at Joseph's beck and call and had kept the restaurant open for us countless times.

"That sounds wonderful," I said, slipping a summer dress over my head and wriggling my toes into a pair of sandals.

"Let's go, love," Joseph whispered to me, planting a final kiss on my lips before making his way to the cockpit. I attempted to bring calmness to my body after our recent conquests.

My eyes swept the darkening runway as dusk settled. Marshaling sticks dotted the landing strip and Joseph pulled in with as much ease as breathing. His sports cars awaited us the moment the plane touched down, prepared ahead of time, just like my hair ribbons in the drawer of the dressing table and the reservation at Chef Georgina's. Joseph was a man who thrived on order and being in complete control.

Joseph left Barry to close up the plane and was by my side

in a moment. In minutes we were in his car and heading into town. Joseph rested his hand on my thigh just under my skirt while we drove. I studied his handsome profile, taking in every line of his face which was set in concentration. This was not just one of his rebellious trips to escape his parents. There was something on his mind. I knew him well and had been able to see it all over him from the moment he stripped his clothes. Joseph had an agenda.

Secretly, I hoped that he was ready to make up his mind about what he wanted, ready to put some of the planning he lent to the other facets of his life into our situation. I wanted him to tell me that he was ready to make me his wife. Lord knew I had been ready to be his for what felt like ages.

A valet took care of Joseph's car and he took my hand as we made our way into the restaurant, holding it a little tighter than usual as if feeling the need to keep me close.

Though we always took the same table, a waiter had been kept late to escort us through the dining room. I knew that Chef would have our order already prepared: fresh seafood salad and crab cakes for me and oysters for Joseph.

I remembered the first time we'd come to Georgina's and he'd urged me to try one of his oysters. I couldn't get past the slime and Joseph had found it endlessly amusing as I was also unable to tolerate swallowing his sperm.

We settled down in the plush booth, the delicious scent of our dinners wafting from the kitchen to tease my senses, especially when I thought of the oysters.

Joseph always looked like a model out of a magazine and I could hardly take my eyes off of him in the candlelight. It was the perfect evening.

Yet, something was off. I'd already gotten the sense and even the hope that he had something momentous to tell me, but the wrinkle across his brow was concerning me. As a man who seemed to so often have the world at his beck and call, I only remembered seeing this expression on his face before a big test in school—never had I seen this look when it came to real-life matters. There was never any need as he always had it all under control.

Joseph broke the silence that had lingered during our drive and arrival at the restaurant by making small talk. I'd been talking for a few minutes straight about the Ford case when he took my hand. It was strange considering the topic of discussion was anything but romantic. I realized then that I had been so wrapped up in what I was talking about that I hadn't even noticed the tenderness on his face. He wasn't listening to what I was saying at all.

I stopped, studying him in an attempt to decipher the affection mingling with the pensiveness on his face.

"Joseph? Are you alright?" I asked.

Uneasiness welled up within me when he squeezed my hand. He offered a smile that held such gentleness it made my heart hurt. These feelings were foreign and I did not care for them. If he was going to suggest we solidify our future together, why did I feel so off-balance?

Joseph held my gaze while he brought my hand to his lips, kissing the fingertips instead of the back of my hand the way an ordinary person would. I became further disconcerted when he looked straight into my eyes. "I love you, Samantha." The declaration was whispered, something Joseph never did because he couldn't care less what anyone thought of whatever he had to say. The extreme tenderness was getting to me.

"I love you too, Joseph, you know that."

For God's sake, Joseph, just get it over with. Tell me you want us to be married, tell me you want me to be your wife...

Of course, Joseph offered me no such relief. Just as he did with his tantalizing teasing in place of foreplay, he kept me foaming at the mouth, waiting for answers, the way he always did.

We finished our dinner, but instead of enjoying the luxury of a handsome man across from me and delicious food in front of me, I couldn't make myself let go like I usually could. Instead, I did my best to get through the rest of dinner, wishing this pensive version of Joseph would be replaced by his usual, laid-back persona so we could be ourselves.

"Thanks, Georgina," I said as we left the restaurant.

"A pleasure, as always," the Chef said, smiling at me. "Joseph."

Joseph offered Georgina only a slight nod, barely pausing as we walked past the man who'd remained open well past 1 AM for us. His hand was on my arm and he directed me with purpose. I was about to rib him for being so rude to the chef and ask if he was anxious to get back to the bedroom, but he pushed me against a brick wall at the front of the restaurant and kissed me before I could speak. Just like everything else that night, it wasn't like his kisses normally were. Instead of strong, forceful, and filled with desire, these were soft, gentle, and loving.

Once again, I opened my mouth to speak, but the valet pulled up with Joseph's car.

Joseph took my hand, wordlessly, leading me to the passenger's side. After getting in he pulled out, gunning the motor the moment we hit the road.

I waited for him to speak, even though I knew he wouldn't. Joseph knew what I needed and he knew how to stretch me thin. Apart from Saul, he knew me better than anyone: the secrets I locked away from the world, the reason for my lack of trust, the past that haunted me. There was no doubt in my mind that he knew he was building anticipation within me. I could only hope that it was to make his words as effective as possible when he asked me to be his wife, his forever.

Building more tension was far from necessary. My hunger for Joseph already overpowered every one of my senses. Still, I longed to hear those words.

When we arrived at the Boca House, every light in the place glowed even though it was 2 AM. The Henley's, caretakers of the house, stood on the front porch ready to receive us.

It was a one-level house, with five bedroom suite's right on the water. The views from the terraces were incredible, it was peaceful and serene to sit and watch the boats go by. The Johnson family owned the rest of the cul-de-sac. This was the grandchildren of the Johnson and Johnson pharmaceutical company.

The family usually lived in Florida most of the time and we were always welcomed guests by them. They usually hosted a dinner party for Joseph and me when we came to Boca. They teased Joseph about making an honest woman out of me. He always responded, "when she's ready", and looked my way as if to put the decision back on me. This time, he would be surprised at my answer, I was ready to be his wife.

Mrs. Henley, tall, outspoken and stern and Mr. Henley short and laid back, were around 65.

Mr. Henley took care of the grounds, the boat, cars, the maintenance on the house, and the koi pond that I loved. Mrs. Henley cleaned and cooked for the family.

My mind was so distracted as we made our way inside that I scarcely remember saying hello to the Henley's so preoccupied were my thoughts of Joseph and me.

I thought of the French doors in our suite at the back of the house that opened up onto a terrace, facing the water and how it would be the perfect place for him to say what he'd been building up to all evening. Or perhaps we would take a late-night excursion down to the water and go skinny dipping like we had so many times. There, he would tell me beneath the moonlight that he wanted to be my husband.

I was taken by surprise, pulled from my reverie when Joseph swept me off my feet and carried me toward our bedroom. He leaned close to my ear. "Samantha, darling." He said it like a breath as if even my name needed to be spoken with tenderness.

I buried my face in his neck, breathing in the lingering smell of the restaurant. I clung to him and the scent that was all his own, gliding my hand into his shirt, running the palms of my hands along this chest.

Joseph carried me right to the bed when we reached our suite, setting me down onto the lush duvet before lowering himself carefully on top of me, his lips did not leave my face for a second.

As always, fruit and red wine were waiting on a table by the king-sized bed. Just as Marge and Barry were accustomed to becoming scarce, Mr. and Mrs. Henley did the same. After their initial welcome, the only sign of their presence became the fact that every detail, down to the gardenia's Mr. Henley arranged in our suite, was in place. However, Joseph didn't show the slightest interest in those things for the moment.

It had been a long day and my eyelids were growing heavy with sleep. Joseph was not finished with me yet. As I hung between wakefulness and imminent slumber, I gave in to his lovemaking.

He took my sandals off and pulled my dress over my head. Now I was exposed, my breasts in a lace bra, straining to be released and my panties were a matching satin. At first, he gazed at my body, drinking in all my curves and beauty. His desire was visible in his eyes. He kissed my lips long and hard. I returned his kiss with equal force. With one hand, he released the hook on my bra, my breasts bounced forward and he cupped them in his hand. He caressed me gently, kissing my ears and neck, down to my stomach. I arched my back, forcing my pelvis forward, a signal that I was ready for his dark penis to enter my pale vagina. He moved slowly, dipping into me. He released his sperm while I screamed in the pleasure of orgasm. He clung to me as if I was going to dissolve under him. We both, exhausted fell asleep still together in our love position. The last thing I remembered was him saying, "I love you."

Chapter 5

The following morning, I blinked my eyes open, sleepily. The after-effects of Joseph's passion from the previous night mingled with satisfaction in my mind. I turned onto my side, watching the steady rise and fall of Joseph's chest as he slept. I drank my fill of pleasure and was fully satiated. Joseph's relaxed state assured me he felt the same.

I stroked my hand along the taut skin of his honeyed chest, knowing that my touch wouldn't wake him and that he'd likely sleep for a couple more hours. Memories of the previous night took form, the desire for me burning on his face, the determined set of his shapely jaw as he had his way with me. Thoughts of pleasure and control moved through my head. Once I'd basked for a few moments in this aftershock of the ecstasy we'd shared, I slid out of bed and padded to the bathroom.

There were sexual excursions between the times Joseph and I became one, but they did nothing to keep me in condition for the rigorous demands of his lovemaking. Joseph was sensitive to this reality and always gave me sufficient time to recover. I had a hunch that he only slept late to give my body adequate rest.

I entered the bathroom, unsurprised to find it stocked with robes, soap, lavender oil, toothpaste, toothbrushes, razors, and shaving cream. I turned on the water in the large bathtub, pouring in a generous amount of lavender oil, dreaming of the soothing effect it would have on my body.

I took my time, adding fresh water to the bath to keep a temperature that pleased me. Once I was finished, I made my way out onto the terrace, swaddled in the fleece robe to enjoy the view. Coffee and my favorite muffins were already waiting.

My mind wandered once again back to the man sleeping in the bedroom—my perfect match intellectually, sexually, and passionately. The only thing besides the disapproval of his parents that kept us apart was the demanding nature of both of our jobs. However, I had finally reached a place in my heart where I would have gladly taken a back seat and focused on furthering Joseph's career. I was ready to become a support for him. He needed only to say the word and I would be his.

My attention turned to the French doors with the sound of footsteps. Joseph came toward me, dressed in running shorts and tennis shoes. I took my time feasting on the sight of his bare chest as he came close enough to drop a kiss on the top of my head.

"Feeling alright?"

Though Joseph knew I needed time to recover from our passionate intercourse, he never mentioned it outright. There was no need to apologize. It was what we both wanted and we knew, regardless of the pain, I would never refuse the chance to become intertwined with him.

I nodded, stretching my arms above my head. "Yes, I'm fine."

"Good. I'm going for a run to clear my head. Be ready to go out to the boat by the time I get back?" I nodded, watching the bronzed splendor of his retreating back as he left our suite. I watched the waterline until I saw him run past, his perfectly sculpted muscles coursing as he ran, reigniting my desire for him. He was a beautiful man. I wanted nothing more than for him to be forever mine.

His words sent my mind into thought once again. Clear his head? That strange feeling that had settled over me last night, that he was trying to work up the right words to tell me something resurfaced. Truth be told, I had been using my time this morning to collect my thoughts. It was natural after the kind of night we'd just had, especially considering it had been months since an encounter. Still, it was a comfort to know that Joseph never brought another woman to the house-Mrs. Henley had told me of that. She'd always liked me and I was pleased that she saw fit to entrust me with this reassurance. Still, concern over the fact that whatever he had to say plagued him so continued to haunt me.

The residual scent of the lavender oil from my bath coupled with the taxing nature of the previous night made me feel drowsy and I dozed off. The dreams I'd been formulating about Joseph and I while I was awake intermingled with the sensations of our night together. I jumped when I heard the door to the suite open. I shook myself, realizing that I'd slept through Joseph's run.

Joseph joined me on the terrace, his skin glazed with sweat, his dark curls in disarray from the wind and still carrying the smell of the ocean. He straddled me where I sat, leaning toward me for a kiss.

"Go shower," I teased, pressing my pointer finger into his chest.

Joseph ignored me, swooping me up into his arms as if I weighed nothing at all and carrying me into the bedroom. He threw me on the bed, stripped off his shorts and kicked off his tennis shoes, pulled the belt loose that held my robe closed and now we were both naked, just what he wanted. I told him I would be ready to go when he got back, but Joseph seemed far more pleased with the fact that I was still in my robe, making my body easily accessible to him once again. Nothing mattered, Joseph would have what he wanted, and with me on my back, he kissed me hard. I no longer minded his sweat, he had aroused that tingling between my legs. He looked at me with those dark eyes and thrust himself into me. "Open your eyes" he command. "I want to see those big, blue eyes."

I obeyed and we locked eyes as he brought us to climax together. Three passionate thrusts and we had reached our peak. Then, he kissed me long and hard.

"Join me in the shower, sweetheart?" he asked. I nodded my head and he scooped me up. We finished our morning fun washing each other in the shower.

By the time we were done in the shower, it was late. We dressed quickly and made our way downstairs to collect the lunch Mrs. Henley had prepared. Just as Barry kept things running smoothly on the jet, Greg handled things on the boat.

Joseph never asked if I wanted to go out to sea, he already knew that I would follow him anywhere, same as he knew I would clear my hectic schedule to accommodate him. It was my fate—one that I would happily embrace for the rest of my days.

The air on the water was perfect, whipping across my face. I watched as Joseph and Greg manned the boat, enjoying how the sun illuminated Joseph's dark skin and hair. Imagine the gorgeous children we would make, a perfect blend of us.

"Samantha, darling?"

I turned my eyes to him with a ready smile. "Hey."

Joseph wrapped his arms around me from behind. He took my earlobe between his teeth, nibbling softly for a few moments. "Where were you? Far away it seemed."

I pressed my back in closer to him, the rock of the boat moving easily along with the sway of our bodies. I turned my head to capture his lips. He held my gaze for a few long moments, making it impossible to look away. The wrinkle of concern returned to his face when I stepped back to the railing. My contemplation of a future together had gone so deep that I knew it was time to bring up his pensive behavior.

"May I point out that I'm not the only one who seems far away?" I said, my voice soft. A look that I couldn't quite identify flashed across Joseph's face, but he remained silent.

I reached up to run my hand along his freshly shaven face, tracing his upper lip with my index finger. "Something is going on in your mind, I know you."

Joseph averted his eyes, reaching up to grasp my hand in his own.

"Tell me now. No secrets, remember?"

Back in law school we had promised each other that we would never try to hide the truth, that we would be transparent. No matter what.

Joseph's eyes darkened with intensity as he pulled me in for another kiss and whispered, almost inaudibly that he loved me. The pulse in his neck as he cradled my head near his collar bone hammered in my ear.

"You're scaring me, Joseph," I murmured, my body tensing.

Joseph pulled back from me, turning toward the rail, grasping it until his knuckles turned white.

I started to wish I hadn't pressed the subject. His reaction made me feel I wasn't ready to hear what he had to say. What was coming couldn't be good. Not for me....not for us. The intuitive dread from dinner was resurfacing. I felt certain that my worst fears were about to be confirmed even though I'd woven together the opposite in my thoughts. Just because I imagined them didn't mean that they would come to fruition.

"I have something to tell you," he started, slowly. "It's going to change my plans for us. For now." My throat closed, causing it to ache for lack of air. He had been making plans for us. Yet, now that I knew, he was saying that they were not to be?

"Eight weeks ago, my parents invited me to their home to welcome some of their friends who were visiting from South Africa. When I was a child, their daughter, Emily and I used to play together while our parents talked. Both her parents and mine had always hoped that we would grow fond of each other, fall in love, and end up married. My parents were fans of the notion because Emily's parents are prominent in the DC circuit and it would have been advantageous for all involved. However, this never happened as she, like me, had different plans for her life and disregarded the preferences of her mother and father in personal matters."

Joseph shifted his weight, keeping his eyes on everything except me. "I forgot all about Emily. I met you and I was sure that I could never love another woman like this."

I folded my arms, suddenly feeling cold. "Was she with

them?" I guessed, dread continuing to accumulate within me.

Joseph hesitated for a moment before nodding. "Samantha, you're my best friend, my lover, my whole heart. I would never want to hurt you."

No...please, no...

"During the visit," Joseph pressed on. "Emily and I decided to go for a horseback ride to escape our parents for a while. We ended up spending some time at the back of my father's barn."

The questioning look on my face caused Joseph to go on. "We'd been drinking and were far past tipsy."

I drew in a deep breath. "Okay."

"We were determined to go riding, but that seemed pretty much impossible considering the state we were in. From there, we started to mess around."

I angled away from him, bracing myself.

"Samantha. "

The gentle pleading in his voice did nothing to soften the feelings raging within me. I was trembling now and Joseph reached out a hand to touch me. I moved away, waiting for the rest.

"She knows how I feel about you," Joseph said. "And she was engaged to a man from South Africa."
The word *was* sent off warning bells in my head.

"She knew that my plan was always to be with you. But I

don't know..." He trailed off.

I chanced a look at him. "Yes, you do." My voice sounded wounded even to my ears.

Joseph ran a hand through his hair, exhaling. "We were both lonely," he said. "She kissed me and started taking off my clothes. It was too tempting."

Marcus dared to worm his way back into my thoughts then. I had been intimate with him as well. Joseph wasn't the only one who had been with another. I knew that this wasn't all he had to say. There had to be more because if that was it, the words wouldn't have been so hard for him to bring forth.

"You said she was engaged, is it you she wants to marry now?" I asked, my tone leaving no doubt of the pain inflicted upon me.

"She's pregnant, Samantha."

The whirlwind ceased and became replaced by a crushing force. It was hard to convince myself that a literal load hadn't fallen upon my shoulders. I thought of the passionate manner in which we'd made love, then the tenderness. How could he? I'd expected whatever was causing him such trepidation would not be easy, but this was far worse, far more traitorous than I had anticipated.

I had planned to be in his arms by now, below deck, making love and then sleeping peacefully in his arms, resting completely in the fact that he was mine alone. Instead, my worst nightmare was being fleshed out before me in the most brutal of terms.

It wasn't as if I was ignorant of the possibility. Our love and emotions had always been for one another exclusively, but no restrictions had been placed upon satisfying our own carnal, physical needs with others. Yet, the reality that he had let this happen with anyone besides me hit hard.

"Our family's feel disgraced, betrayed," Joseph said.

They feel betrayed?! And what about me, Joseph?

"Emily's engagement is off. The only way is for us to marry." Joseph began pacing the deck. Sweat had appeared beneath his linen shirt.

"According to your parents?" I prompted. "Or according to you?"

Joseph moved towards me and grasped my arms. "Samantha, I need to take care of Emily and my baby. It doesn't have to mean anything less for us. It would be a marriage in name only."
My mind stumbled over itself, trying to process the words he had spoken. I tried to picture Joseph with a wife and a child. He said eight weeks ago. Painfully, I realized, he remembered the exact number because that was how far along Emily was in her pregnancy. He would be forever tied to another woman, never completely mine.

The hole being drilled into my heart became deeper with each passing moment as the news continued to sink, suffocating me. No longer able to stand the conflict etched on his face, I attempted to flee from Joseph. My legs gave out beneath me and I crumpled to the ground. The weight of his words was too much. As my mind spun, I felt Joseph's presence. Although he was physically there, his voice sounded distant. The hands touching my body were void of their usual electricity. I felt nothing. Cold, despondent nothing.

Chapter 6

I woke slowly, my eyelids stinging from residual tears, the corners crusty like sand. I stared blankly at the wall, feeling the gentle rocking of the boat.

It had been a terrible dream. Joseph was about to bind himself forever to another woman. Someone else was going to have his child. He had betrayed me.

A sob broke in my throat once I became fully awake and realized this was no dream. It was my tragic reality.

I sat up cautiously, my body feeling fragile, though, for once, intense orgasming had nothing to do with it. This ache wasn't satisfying—it was painful and I felt as delicate as a piece of fine china.

Even though he sat wordlessly, I could feel Joseph's presence in the room. My eyes turned to him and our gazes locked. For a few moments, we rested in a kind of stand-off, as we each waited for the other to speak. Joseph broke first.

"How are you feeling?"

I wanted to shout at him for having the audacity to ask such a question when he'd just stolen my life, my hopes, and my dreams from me. I angled my body away from him, wrapping my arms around myself.

Joseph stood. "I need to explain."

I remained quiet, listening as his footsteps came closer. "Samantha, you know that I love you—" "Do I?" I spat, finally finding my voice. "How could I know that, Joseph? When you would give away a vital part of yourself to someone else and kill any future for us. You practically demote me to your mistress and then expect me to believe that you love me? I may not know much about true love, but I do know that this is not it."

Joseph was already shaking his head and making his way toward me. I pulled the sheets to my chest. "Don't come near me."

"Please." His voice was strained. He sat down on the bed but made no further indication that he would touch me. The silence stretched out between us. It felt like ages and with each passing moment. The sense of betrayal he'd heaped upon me only grew thicker and more capable of swallowing me whole.

"Samantha," he finally said. "Listen. The only reason we are going to be married is because of Emily's parents. They are ashamed that she is with child out of wedlock."

"Responsible." I stared incredulously at him and grew even angrier when his face registered only confusion. "You just don't get it, do you?"

"Baby, I do, really. It's just that this is what needs to be done for now. After a few years, Emily and I will mutually agree to annul the marriage."

"You've already agreed to this?" I asked.

Joseph hesitated, causing the knot in my stomach to tighten. "No, but as much as I wish to be with you, Emily wishes to be with the man she has given her heart to. My plans for us will not be affected, only postponed."

Scorned

I stared at him, wishing that I could believe his words. However, reason would not allow it.

"There is no guarantee that you will both feel the same years from now. Marriage isn't like sleeping around. It's more permanent. Perhaps that's why you never found it in your heart to propose to me after all these years."

I could tell that my words were doing a number on Joseph's emotions and I was glad. He deserved to experience the same pain, to suffer as I did.

"I love you, Samantha. You are the only one I will ever love."

His declaration threatened to penetrate my shield but was not quite potent enough. It occurred to me then how fully one traitorous act could suck the meaning out of such words. My eyes drilled into the blanket covering me and my whole body pulsed. If this had never happened, we would have been making love beneath it.

"Please, baby. Let me hold you."

I shook my head. "I want to go home. Just take me home. Now."

I refused to lift my gaze, but after a pause, I felt Joseph stand and heard his footsteps as he left me alone.

I heard Joseph radioing Barry, telling him to have the jet ready. Then he called Saul. I sought to block the sound of their conversation out by falling back asleep. Desperately, I wanted to sleep through this nightmare, but even when slumber came, I was to be plagued by the nightmare that had become my life.

By the time I realized I was in Joseph's arms, I completely lacked the strength to fight him.

Begrudgingly, I allowed my head to rest against his chest. I didn't lift it until I heard Saul's voice.

"Saul!" I couldn't control the trembling of my mouth and the quiver in my voice. Saul took me immediately.

"Samantha," Joseph said. "Let me go with you. I'll make sure you arrive in New York safely."

They were hardly the words I wanted to hear from the man who had just damaged me beyond repair.

"Good-bye, Joseph," Saul said.

The next thing I knew we were on the plane. I took one last look outside, the view very much the same as when Joseph and I set off on our romantic getaway. The difference was this time Joseph stood alone watching us prepare to take off. I could tell that he was crying, but it didn't bring me to tears. My emotions were drained for the time being. I was ready to go home.

I remembered little of the plane ride, being transported from the plane to the limo. I asked to go to Rick and Scott's apartment and Saul obliged. I slept as soon as my head hit the pillow. The men watched over me.

When I awakened in a strange bedroom, I was ready to panic. If Rick hadn't entered when he did, I might have.

"Hello, sunshine," he said, affectionately.

I sat up, rotating my neck in an attempt to relieve the

tightness. "W-what happened?" I felt shaky and weak.

"You've been here for a couple of days," Rick said. The tray he carried contained water and a slice of toast with butter.

"No coffee?" I teased, as he'd been preparing my coffee every morning for many years.

"I think it's better to take it easy for the moment and coffee might make you jittery. You're here to relax, convalesce, feel better."

Rick, always there to see to my every need, no matter how others abused me. "Uh-huh." I took one bite of the toast and downed the water, having just realized how dry my throat felt.

"I need a shower," I said.

"Of course," Rick responded, standing.

I was confused when he immediately moved to help me, but the moment I stood on my feet, I understood. My knees nearly gave out and I leaned heavily on Rick as we made our way to the ensuite bathroom.

I sat on the toilet and started to undress. Everything Joseph said came rushing to my brain. I had to wash the memories away, I turned the shower on and let the water trickle over me. Tears escaped me once more. Why had life given me this beautiful man and now taken him from me? I began to lather my hair and wash my body. The last man that entered me was Joseph. I vigorously scrubbed between my legs to wash his essence away. After I finished, I dried off and put on the robe Rick had laid out for me.

I entered the dining room, greeted by Scott and the meal he crafted for me. A pasta dish decorated with brightly colored butternut squash, spinach, and a light sauce. Comfort food that would not disrupt my delicate system.

I must have looked like a little, lost girl. My hair was a tangled wet mess, the robe was oversized, and my face was bare. I knew Rick and Scott did not care about my appearance.

"How are you?" Scott asked, offering me a kind smile.

I felt tears welling up, but it seemed as if my faucet had run out and none came to the surface. "I've been better."

"You need to take it easy," Scott said. "You haven't been well."

I sampled the delicious-looking meal that Scott had placed before me, but I tasted nothing. It was as if every one of my senses had been dulled.

The phone rang for me. It was Saul. He had just left this morning to change his clothes. Saul assured me he would see me later and we hung up.

"I'm going back to work," I said once Rick had rejoined me. He paused, studying me from across the table. "Are you sure?" I nodded. "Work will help. I need something to put my mind to." "Yes, I can understand that," he answered.

I took another forkful of pasta, chewing slowly. It felt so foreign I wondered how long it had been since I'd eaten solid food.

"Joseph has contacted us several times," Rick went on, his tone careful as if I were a fragile child and any word might set me off on a tantrum. I felt like a child now, so I didn't blame him for choosing his words carefully. They stung, but this experience had debilitated me for long enough and I wanted to be caught up on what had transpired around me.

"What did he have to say?"

Rick toyed with the linen napkin beside his plate. "He told me that he is going to do everything in his power to make this up to you—that he loves you."

I stared at my plate of uneaten food, processing these words, the ones that had meant next to nothing on the boat and meant just as little now.

"I'll return to work tomorrow." With that, I stood, leaving the dining room.

Chapter 7

Work had piled up since I was gone. I threw myself into it, sometimes spending the night at the office. I needed to hire another attorney, but I had not found the right match yet. I filled my mind with contracts, variances, labor disputes, anything to not think of Joseph.

I had gotten very thin and everyone was worried about my health. There were fleeting moments of lovesickness, but other than that, I felt fine. Fine was not the right word but that was the word I continued to use. I was fine.

Saul was the most worried and he stayed a few nights with me at my apartment. I tried to share my feelings with him but Joseph was too painful for me to talk about. I knew Joseph called Saul, Rick, and Scott to check on me, but I did not ask about him, nor did I want to talk to him. I read that he had married in a quiet family ceremony in DC. The wedding did not get the coverage that someone of his family's importance would normally receive. Most likely, this was because of the baby. Joseph's family would do anything to avoid scandal. Neither Emily nor Joseph looked very happy.

The small traces of softness I had towards men, Joseph had cultivated and then destroyed. When I fell asleep I could feel my desire to overpower any man who dared get in my way, harden like lead in my chest. It was a familiar feeling. A feeling that assured me I was falling back into my old patterns, the ones Joseph had nearly rescued me from.

Tears did not spring from my eyes when I heard the news of the ceremony. I still felt sensitive, but the sting was dulled by reviving my old toughness.

I took to spending the night at my office. I worked until my mind gave way to the oblivion of sleep. On one such night, when my brain had reached its full capacity for work-related material, I dared to contemplate beyond Joseph's marriage and into his reasons.

As I stood in front of the large window in my office, looking out over the lights in the city, in the furthest recesses of my mind I found it within myself to understand why Joseph had decided to marry Emily. There would be no issue with a biracial child-the future of the baby would be secure once its parents became a proper couple. Though I wished Joseph had been more responsible when he decided to mess around with Emily, how could I fault him for wanting to do the right thing afterward? A dull ache filled me, replacing the part that had once been occupied by passion.

Joseph had given to another what was supposed to be ours together. This betrayal would linger, I was sure. When I considered my own past, I could momentarily believe what Joseph had said.

I was the only one for him and there would never be another...

My mind moved to thoughts of Kenneth. Hadn't my own brief experience with pregnancy stemmed from careless intercourse, oneness with a person who meant nothing to me?

After my night with Kenneth, there was a casual conversation of "doing this kind of thing again" but it was unlikely we'd become fixtures in one another's lives considering the superficial nature of our encounter.

I was in a state of denial when I became violently sick to my stomach a month later. Retaining any link to Kenneth beyond the gratification of momentary sexual desire was inconceivable. I told myself that it was nothing more than the flu. By the afternoon I was healthy and then sick again the next morning. It became increasingly difficult to deny the implications. After a week of throwing up every morning, I threw in the towel. It was finally time to visit the doctor.

I'd never been fond of hospitals. To this point in my life, I'd been very healthy so I was practically a stranger to my OBGYN. The woman hadn't even performed a PAP smear on me due to my absence from routine appointments. Suddenly being tested for pregnancy when I hadn't been examined in years was surreal. Part of me was still convinced that there was no way my symptoms had anything to do with Kenneth. They couldn't!

I felt numb throughout the entire exam.

"I'm just going to have Miriam draw your blood, alright, Samantha?" the doctor finally said after the seemingly unremarkable check-up.

Just take it all, I thought as the fear that something might show up on the test settled in my lungs once again.

The student nurse, who looked like she'd never made a mistake in her life, joined the exam room, took my blood, and then disappeared for thirty minutes.

I had begun to shiver uncontrollably and was trying desperately to stop when the virtuous Miriam knocked on the door. The look on her face made me wish I had locked the door, though it would do little to change the test results.

"Hi, Samantha, " she said, sitting down on the cushioned stool in front of me. I couldn't bear the sympathy on her unworldly face. "You're pregnant. "

I remained silent, unable to summon a single word.

"I assume you didn't plan this, " the nurse went on.

Of course, you're making assumptions. That's what you girls who never fuck up do.

I'd never been so annoyed with someone who was trying desperately to fill the void of silence. "I've set up an appointment for you with Planned Parenthood. Does next week work alright?" I went through the motions of answering questions as thoughts of Kenneth sped through my consciousness, mocking me, worrying me, making me wonder what on earth I'd allowed.

I felt as if I'd been released from a prison cell when I finally stepped out of the cold, sterile doctor's office. I made my way down the equally impersonal, white hallways and outside into the world where life went on. Though I'd been released, the sinking reality that all of my troubles were coming with me was inescapable.

I sat in my car, dreading what was ahead, but knowing what I had to do. And so, I began a series of phone calls.

First on the list was my close friend, Tony. She was my confidant in every aspect of life. I could fully turn to her with even the worst of my troubles. Considering this was the worst scrape I'd ever been in, I dialed her number without hesitation.

Comfort enveloped me at the mere sound of her voice.

"Hey, stranger, " she said. I could hear the smile behind the

words. "Been a long time." "Hi, Tony. "

"Is something wrong? "

It had always been impossible to conceal my worry from her as she'd developed a sixth sense that seemed to give her heightened awareness of my needs.

"I'm pregnant. "

"Oh, god, Samantha."

Silence reigned for a few moments and I could hear the blinker ticking in her car. " Who 's the guy?" she finally asked. "Kenneth." "The barfly? "

"Gosh, Tony, please don't call him that," I said, pressing two fingers to my throbbing temple. "Why not?"

"Because I want to believe he'll help me out with this. I need to believe that there is some sort of responsibility within this man."

"Are you at home?"

"Not yet."

"Alright, head there now. I'll be there in 20 minutes."

I drove home, arriving before my friend. Immediately, I changed into sweats and the warmest sweater I had, but the added warmth did nothing to eliminate the shakes which had returned full-force.

Tony arrived in record time. She was dressed in her usual business attire, looking so in-control and put together, the way I typically did. She wordlessly let herself in and dropped her purse on the *counter. Then she made a beeline toward me.*

"I'm surprised you don't have a glass of wine yet," Tony said, half-joking though the seriousness never left her face. She settled in the overstuffed chair across from me, slipping her feet out of her high-heeled work shoes.

"I think I'd need something far stronger than wine to gain any relief in this situation. Unfortunately, drugs aren't exactly advisable when you're pregnant." My attempt at humor also fell flat as I felt tears pressing against the backs of my eyes.

Tony studied me for a moment. Instead of trying to fill the silence with meaningless words, she'd always been the type to wait, allowing me to direct the conversation when I was ready. To have someone listen to my plight helped some.

"What would you do if you were me?" I asked.

"You mean, what did I do when I was you?" Tony corrected.

I stared at my friend, unable to comprehend the reference. "You were…Pregnant?" I ventured, still unable to fully process the idea.

Tony nodded. "It was a long time ago."

I let this sink in for a moment before continuing. "What did you do?" "I had an abortion."

There was rarely a time when Tony was unruffled, but the flicker of pain behind her eyes at the memory momentarily broke her composure.

"Do you think you did the right thing?" I asked, my voice barely audible.

Tony shrugged. "Yes. What else could I do? I knew that the man wasn't going to be in the picture, so I had little choice. "

"That's what I am afraid of," I said.

Tony leaned closer to me, looking straight into my eyes. "Listen, Samantha. This Kenneth creature isn't going to care a single whit about the baby. Trust me, you're not going to get any support from him."

"So, what would you have me do? Not even tell him?"

Tony nodded. "There's no need. It's better to just make a decision. You're on your own as far as he is concerned, believe me. "

"I guess abortion is the only way, huh? " I said.

Tony nodded. "I know it isn't easy to think about, but you have to consider what it would be like to try and keep the child. You'd be sacrificing your career, everything."

If the abortion was the right thing to do, I wondered why the very thought made it impossible to breathe.

"I'll go with you, Samantha. "

I nodded, slowly, trying my hardest to push aside the unsettled feeling. Could I morally terminate the baby without the father's knowledge?

Once Tony had left, I still wasn't convinced that taking such a drastic course of action without Kenneth was the right thing.

At last, I decided to tell him. Though Kenneth had no children *of his own and was practically a stranger to me, I hoped that he would at least take slight responsibility for his actions. I chose to disregard Tony's warning and give him a chance.*

I was sorely mistaken. As Tony had guessed, he was completely insensitive, shattering the tenuous hope I'd held that he would make the situation more bearable. Instead, he seemed determined to make it as painful as possible.

"Just cut it out, " he said, his voice devoid of emotion. "It 's nothing more than a tumor. " For the first time since learning about the baby, I found myself mute. "

"What?"

Kenneth demanded, sharply. "You can't be worried about money? I'll pay for it." "That's it? " I stammered.

It was.

Waiting six weeks to have the abortion was even worse than telling Kenneth. The fetus needed to be big enough so that they could be sure they'd scraped all of it out.

Scrape away the life growing within me...as if it were nothing at all.

When I returned from these remembrances, I found myself sitting on the floor of my office, trembling at how real reliving those experiences had felt.

This feeling was the reason I had kept my mind from going there. I desperately wished I could go back once again, return to my hardened state. Painful as it had been, this feeling was worse. My desire to undo what Joseph had done, to have Joseph once again to myself was strong. Yet, would I wish for his child to suffer the same fate as mine? Would I wish that kind of grief on anyone even in light of my present pain? Joseph was much too honorable to wipe out human life. He would never expect Emily to do away with the result of their actions, careless as they may have been.

I stumbled back to my desk, my bleary gaze returning to the Mason file that was spread out before me. The words swam before my eyes. I wasn't sure if the sensation came from tears or my overtired state. I gave up after only a moment, laying my head down, wishing for nothing more than to escape my mind.

Chapter 8

It felt as if the sound of knocking went on forever before I found the will to peel my eyes open. I sat up, blinking in confusion at my office door. My hair was a frizzy mess around my face. I could tell that my make-up smudged because of the charcoal-black marks on my arms. Everything felt sticky. Had I been crying? I couldn't remember.

"Come in," I called without even thinking to ask who it was. Fortunately, it was only Rick.

My assistant acted as if nothing were amiss, bringing in a pot of coffee, speaking to me the same way he would if I donned a freshly-pressed suit and had just arrived for work.

"Good morning," he said, pouring me a cup and offering sugar and cream.

I muttered a response, running my hands through my hair, stretching my shoulders which I feared would retain permanent kinks from being habitually hunched over my desk.

"How are you?"

"Fine." It was the response I'd been giving everyone. Sometimes I felt okay and others I felt extremely sick. It was easier to simply say, fine.

There was no indication that Rick didn't believe me. He continued with a hand placed on my shoulder. "Marcus is on line two."

My cup stopped halfway to my mouth as I looked up at him in bewilderment. "Something about the winter ball," Rick filled in, gently.

I set down my coffee cup, pressing the fingers of one hand to my forehead. Saul had graciously canceled prior plans with Marcus on behalf of my precarious emotional state. He hadn't made me feel guilty and suggested that Marcus be my date to the biggest fundraiser of the year, the winter ball. I figured he thought I'd be feeling better. Although it had been three months, I didn't feel better and the thought of going to a fundraiser nearly ignited another bout of nausea within me.

"Gosh, I'd forgotten. Okay, I'll take it." I figured if I was going to cancel for the second time he might as well hear it from me directly.

Rick left the room as unobtrusively as he'd entered.

I took a deep breath and picked up the phone. "Hi, Marcus."

"Hey," he said in a tone no other business associate would have dared use with me. "Look who has come back from the dead."

I rolled my eyes, leaning back in my chair, inwardly cursing the persistent pain in my lower back. I guess that this was proof that my attempt to tame a bit of his cockiness had failed. Unless he didn't remember it.

"Rick told me that you called about the winter ball," I said, fully intending to make this conversation short and sweet. Short was my main priority. "I've been swamped with work. Just trying to get things back under control."

Scorned

"Perfectly alright," Marcus responded, congenially. "I'm sorry you had to cancel last time. You must be keeping a heck of a schedule."

I wondered how much he knew about what had transpired. He would have to be buried underground not to have caught wind of Joseph's marriage even without the major coverage.

"Well, anyway, I know that you RSVP'd with Saul and he told me a month or so ago that he wanted to have drinks before the ball. I hope you won't mind if I just come for drinks and then go on my way."

"You don't like dancing?"

I didn't like the probing nature of Marcus's question. "It's a dinner too and I haven't been eating much. Plus, I am looking at piles of work on my desk so..." I knew now that the lack of proper sleep was taking its toll. I wanted to kick myself for having allowed my voice to sound so weak.

Marcus spoke quietly, "So it has been like that, has it?" I had a feeling my momentary slip-up had tipped Marcus off. He was aware that I was not in control. I did not like it.

"We will meet at seven, Marcus and the ball begins at eight." Changing the subject was the quickest way of drawing attention away from my mistake.

"Sounds like a plan." Marcus's voice had returned to its smooth, cocky tenor. I hoped he would quickly forget what I said about not eating much and working non-stop.

"Alright talk to you soon, "I said.

We hung up a moment later. I sat back in my chair, the exhaustion from pretending to be okay, dropped on to me with full force. I had managed to survive for three months, but I wondered how much longer I could live like this before frailty overcame me. It took all the strength I could muster to stand and make my way to the fridge in the corner office. I was suddenly very hungry.

Though I hadn't touched it in months, Rick kept the fridge fully stocked. Even as my stomach groaned, I scanned the contents of the fridge with little enthusiasm. It was as if I'd forgotten how to enjoy food. I finally settled on a carton of milk. I'd been craving a lot of milk lately. Anything stronger didn't sit well with my stomach.

Milk in hand, I sat back down at my desk, becoming lost in my files. Since Joseph, hours I spent working seemed to slip away. I had little ability to guess how much time passed once I started. My mind needed the distraction, so I became fully engrossed with work.

I jumped when there was a sudden knock on my office door. After consulting the wall clock, I realized two hours had passed without distraction. Had I missed the sound of the intercom telling me that I had a visitor?

"Come in," I called. My skin went cold when, to my surprise, Marcus confidently strode into my office. "What the?"

Rage stirred within me as I stumbled to form a more intelligible sentence. "How did you get past the receptionist?" I demanded when I managed to find my voice.

Marcus continued to linger leisurely in the doorway, unbothered by my disheveled state. He shrugged at my question, encompassing all of the arrogance of his class in one move. "Charm and devilishly good looks can accomplish more than you would believe."

In spite of myself, a smile crept across my lips. The arrogance was still present, but I liked hearing him address this trait head-on.

"I told you I would go to the ball," I said. How dare he come bursting into my office unannounced? Cocky didn't seem like a strong enough word anymore considering the liberties Marcus thought himself entitled to. Still, the sight of him had brought me more feeling than I'd had since Joseph's betrayal.

"I'm not here about the ball."

I stared at him, my brows rising. "Then do you mind telling me to what I owe the pleasure?" I asked sarcastically.

"Samantha," Marcus said looking me straight in the eye. My name came off his lips with such tenderness that I wondered if he'd practice. Perhaps it sounded that way the night I had brought him into complete submission. The sound brought back a hazy memory...

Before I had a chance to speak, Marcus sauntered over to sit across from me.

"Don't tell me this is what you consider an acceptable lunch."

I glanced at my half-empty carton of milk, scowling at him. "So, what if it is?" I retorted, hanging on to my cold resolve by the skin of my teeth.

"Then I would say it is time for an intervention."

The part of me that clung to the ways of old Samantha was offended by his presumptuousness. Yet, just when I thought there was no softness left, I felt the urge to accept his concern. I kept my eyes diverted, pretending to study the file on my desk.

Marcus leaned toward me, "You need a proper lunch."

I ignored him.

Marcus shut the file I feigned interest in, forcing my eyes to meet his. There was a look on his face, was it compassion? It was a look that made my throat tighten. I held close to my last shred of stubbornness but I was losing the battle.

"Don't take this the wrong way," Marcus said, his voice soft, "But you look like hell."

I folded my arms across my chest, turning my head away once again. Marcus reached across the desk, capturing my jaw in the palm of his hand, forcing my gaze back to his.

"Listen, I'm not going to take no for an answer. I already talked to Rick and he said that you are free to have the entire day off."

I did my best to appear defiant. "Since when do you and Rick plan my schedule?" The sharpness of my words did nothing to change the look of tenderness on Marcus's face.

"You have to eat. Samantha. I've already had groceries delivered to your apartment. All you need to do is say yes to a lovely dinner prepared by your favorite client."

I was a bit unnerved that he knew where I lived, but for a man in his position, finding such detail was as easy as breathing. My stubborn expression did nothing to deter Marcus.

"You have the rest of the day off anyway, so what's your hesitation?"

I paused, hardly able to believe that his tactics were working on me. However, if I was honest with myself, I was feeling increasingly brittle with each passing moment. Food sounded healing. How nice it would be if I managed to stomach the food once it was in front of me and then get some rest. I was so tired.

With a slight nod, I finally acquiesced. I was grateful that Marcus simply stood and motioned toward the door, inviting me to proceed out of the office with slight dignity. Neither Marcus nor I uttered a single word as we rode the elevator down to the lobby where Marcus's Lamborghini was parked. I found it within myself to feel amused by what would have been like if he had opted for the motorcycle today. This was quickly washed away and fatigue overcame me. Marcus opened the passenger's side door, helping me in and buckling the seat belt. I felt like a child.

Marcus allowed me to regain some measure of control once we arrived at my apartment. I pulled out my keys to let us into the secured entrance. From there, we moved to the elevators and punched the button for the 12th floor. The door to my unit opened when we reached the top. I stood in the doorway, looking around my apartment. I hardly recognized it but felt grateful that the maid continued to clean despite my constant absence.

I stayed put while Marcus moved around the apartment. He was more comfortable in the space than I was. As he made his way to the bathroom and began to draw me a bath, it dawned on me.

Marcus was one of those people who genuinely cared.

Whether it was true or not was another matter entirely. But, for the moment, I felt looked after. Similarly to when Saul watched over me after Joseph, I was completely tended to. Frankly, I did not know what to do with it.

Marcus helped make it clear when he reentered the room. He took my hand and led me toward the bathroom. Steam began to fog up the mirrors and the distinct scent of vanilla emanated from the tub. I soaked for a long time, allowing the steam in the air to fill my lungs. I could breathe clearly again. My suffocation was over.

The sounds of knuckles rapping softly on the door finally coaxed my eyes open. Marcus stood in the doorway.

"Dinner will be ready in five minutes, alright?" he smiled gently.

I nodded feeling groggy from the warmth of the water. My entire being was relaxed in a way it hadn't known since Joseph. I carefully exited the tub, drying off and wrapping up in the robe that was waiting for me. A few pins helped clip up my wet hair and with that, I padded into the kitchen.

The counter was covered in fresh herbs, vegetables, and a Cornish hen waiting in the center. Although I hadn't been hungry for weeks, my mouth began to water. Marcus turned away from the stove, sending me a boyish smile over his shoulder, "I hope you're hungry."

"It smells amazing," I stepped closer to look at the perfectly cooked hen. "How did you learn to cook so well?" For a construction man born into the lap of luxury, professional culinary skills were unexpected.

"My mom taught me," Marcus answered, setting a bowl of steaming hot vegetables on the table. "I took to it right away and it has been sort of a secret passion. Come sit down."

I willed my feet to move, but I couldn't manage it. The normalcy of the conversation Marcus made coupled with his gentle presence caused me to crack. I took a few steps back toward the bedroom, "I'm sorry Marcus, I'm just not hungry." I covered my face, attempting to hide that I was losing control of the emotions I'd been stockpiling for months. Marcus took one look at me and soon, I was wrapped in his arms. The dam burst inside of me, causing uncontrollable sobbing. Marcus just held tighter.

Eventually, he picked me up and carried me to a seat in the living room where he cradled me on his lap. After an hour, my tears gave way to sleep. Marcus held me awhile longer and then took me to bed. He pulled back the covers and, with great care, tucked me in.

He kissed my forehead and said, "My sweet girl, I will see you tomorrow."

"Marcus," I said, "I do not want to be alone, will you lay beside me?" "Of course, my darling."

True to his word, he laid on top of the covers. He continued to hold me while I slept, still fully dressed. Dinner was forgotten.

When I awoke from the nap, I felt more rested and at peace

than I had in a long time. Marcus left to clean the dishes and returned to the bedroom to tell me goodnight.

"Marcus, please stay with me tonight. Make love to me. I want to feel again."

With that, he removed his clothes and got into bed immediately. "Darling are you sure?" The feel of his naked body next to mine made words unnecessary.

His body was pressed up to mine. I started to become aroused and I knew he was too, but he would wait for me to make the first move. I turned to face him, "Kiss me please, make me feel you."

He leaned forward and kissed me fully. Tremors shook my body from his lips' caress. He gradually kissed down my neck, working his way toward my supple breasts. He cupped my behind and pulled me to him. His penis was hard, erect, and ready to penetrate. Rather than plunge into me, he made me wait. His hand slowly stroked my clitoris. I began to moan and push my body up to his.

"Samantha, are you sure?"

"I need to feel you inside me."

Marcus did not need a second invitation. He rubbed his erection across the lips of my vagina. I opened wide and he pushed into me with gentle strength. First, his movements were slow, tantalizing. He increased his speed and intensity. Back and forth, in and out he danced until we reached climax simultaneously.

It was gentle sex. Marcus gave it to me just the way I wanted.

I could feel our mingling wetness, the stickiness of his sperm. He kissed me and cupped a hand around my breast. Here, it rested as we slept.

I awoke, for the first time in months, feeling rested, Marcus was on his stomach still asleep. I wanted him again. I kissed his back.

"Good morning," I said. "I am hungry."

He turned over and pulled me on top of him. The covers fell, exposing our nakedness. I was straddling him, his erection already inside of me. This time I rode until we reached our peak. He went rigid and pulled me down to his chest to hold me.

"Good morning, darling," Marcus whispered, stroking my hair with one hand while rubbing my back with the other. "How did you sleep?"

I laid my head on his chest. "Better than I have slept in a long time," I said. "Thank you for staying with me."

"Of course."

We were silent for a few minutes before Marcus propped himself up on one elbow, his hand going to my chest as he fondled one of my breasts. His fingers traced me with remarkable tenderness. He took his hand away briefly to observe, studying me almost reverently before he went back to touching.

Similar to the way Marcus had allowed me to initiate intercourse, waiting until I was ready to give all of myself, he let me speak in my own time. His patience was empowering. I felt comfortable talking about matters I hadn't put to rest since

Joseph's betrayal.

"How could he do that, Marcus?" I whispered under my breath.

Marcus leaned close to kiss my forehead. "I don't know, honey," he said. His breath was warm on my cheek. "He probably doesn't even know the answer to that question himself."

I wasn't sure if this meant he learned about the events from the news or if he had somehow been able to sense the source of my pain. Either way, I didn't care. All I knew was that his understanding and love was the perfect cure. Feelings of safety finally seemed possible to reach with him beside me.

I told him everything.

He held me while I voiced the betrayal, heartache, sadness, anger, and numbness I'd wrestled with for months. I told him how I hadn't been able to escape from it, no matter what I tried. Until then. Until I found his arms.

Marcus looked deep into my eyes for a moment before reaching for his phone. A moment later, I heard the sound of the opera we'd listened to on our first encounter. My eyes grew large in surprise, my mouth popping open as I wondered if he actually remembered the details of our first night. I didn't have the chance to ask because he captured my lips, whisking me away into a whirlwind of lovemaking once again.

Chapter 9

I sat at the table in my bathrobe, watching Marcus prepare breakfast. It was impossible not to admire the gluteus muscles straining against his boxer shorts. I stirred a spoonful of sugar into my coffee, savoring the taste. Months had passed since I'd been able to stomach it.

"My lady," Marcus said, setting a plate in front of me with a courtly flourish.

"You're a magician," I joked, though I wasn't talking about the way he turned the uneaten dinner into a beautiful breakfast. The wicked grin across his face was evidence he understood. Maintaining a smile, he poured himself a fragrant cup and sat down across from me. As I looked at him, I marveled at the reason I'd ended up in his bed in the first place and how it felt to have such a strong connection to him now. Little by little, he was making me believe that, perhaps, healing wasn't quite as distant as I'd thought.

We ate our breakfast for a few minutes before Marcus asked if I wanted more coffee. "Yes, please." I tucked back into my omelet, looking up, realizing Marcus was still by my side.

He bent down, placing a kiss on my forehead. He set the coffee pot down, placing his hands on either side of my chair, boxing me in. "How would you like to spend the day together?"

To have him all to myself, I couldn't think of anything I wanted more. "I'd love to." Marcus gave me a long kiss.

"What should we do?" I asked when we broke apart. "Do

you ice skate?" "Sure."

"Great. I know the perfect place."

Once we'd finished breakfast, I dressed in warm clothes and we swung by Marcus's apartment to get him some new ones.

Marcus cupped my thigh in his hand as we drove. We talked about everything and nothing like real lovers until we made it to an outdoor rink. We rented skates and took to the ice like kids enjoying the first freeze of the winter.

I was an excellent skater, but Marcus was even better.

"You're a man of many talents, Marcus," I said.

He smiled. "I've spent many hours on the rink with my little sisters." "They're lucky," I remarked.

Marcus's expression grew fond. "They're 24 now, but they were born ten years after me. My dad was in his late 60's by then. They were kind of miracles and my parents continue to dote on them to this day because of it."

"I bet you do as well," I teased.

Marcus chuckled. "Nope. Brothers are built to give sisters a hard time. I'm the only one they have, so all the responsibility falls on me. I give them a good share of trouble." He finished with a wink.

I laughed, unable to imagine Marcus being anything but kind and fun-loving with anyone. When we first met, I'd completely missed this side of him. I was so focused on seeing his arrogance. That seemed to have dissipated now and I loved this version of Marcus that I was just getting to know.

"You all sound very close."

Marcus turned to skate backward in front of me. "Yes, we are. Want to meet them?"

I nearly slipped at the suddenness of his words, ordinary though they might seem to any other girl. Though Marcus had quite nearly brought me back to life in a single night, it was hard to grasp the idea of being more than casual, to be special to him.

Something in my chest—was it my heart?—fluttered and I heard myself agree.

Marcus skated around me, stopping hockey-style as he spun me into his arms. He kissed my nose and looked directly at my face. "They'll love you," he whispered.

Though his words were kind, I found myself wishing to hear that he loved me. This thought, surprised me more than Marcus's offer for me to meet his family. I wanted it badly.

After skating, Marcus bought us hot apple cider from a street vendor and we took a carriage around central park. Cuddling up next to him as we rode, the chilly air bit at our faces while the rest of our bodies remained warm. Pressing together was more intoxicating than I could have imagined. I'd felt this way before, but only when having sex. With Marcus, everything became invigorating, even the smallest acts.

As we walked back to his car, I revealed more about what transpired with Joseph. He listened, patiently to every word I spoke. There were no tears this time, only pain. There always would be. However, I had Marcus and I felt safe to live my life. It puzzled me that we could even have a relationship considering the way things started for us. Sexual intrigue and business deals were the initial foundation of our courting.

I was convinced that my longing for more would melt away the moment we returned to my

apartment. And yet, the fact that Marcus invited me out again the following day, assured me it was all real.

Though I was not completely back to 100 percent, I could tell Rick noticed a difference in me. Besides the fact that I hadn't slept on my desktop, I had a feeling the glow inside showed outwardly as well.

Rick didn't mention the change directly, but after so many years of working together, I could read the look on his face. He smiled when he told me that there was food in my refrigerator, obviously able to tell that I'd found my appetite. Eating regular meals brought the color back into my face and my energy was rapidly returning.

It was two weeks after Marcus and I had enjoyed our first full day together and I couldn't stop looking at the clock. The feeling of wanting to dart from my office as soon as 5 o'clock hit was completely foreign to me. Generally, I became so absorbed with work that I stayed well into the evening without realizing it.

Today was different. I couldn't wait to see Marcus. I never seemed to be able to get enough of the warmth and life he brought back into my existence. We were together every day for two weeks and I'd become obsessed. Occasionally, Joseph would creep back into my thoughts and make my head hurt. But the dull ache was soon cured by Marcus's immaculate attention, lively conversation, and incredible intimacy. Sometimes when we went to his apartment to have sex, it was as gentle and slow as the night I'd broken to a million pieces in his embrace. Other times he took me with such force that I was left with bruises. No matter what he gave me, I loved it.

When 5 o'clock hit, I shot from my desk like a schoolgirl at the last bell before summer.

I grabbed my coat and left all of my work in the office. This was routine ever since Marcus and I began occupying all of each other's time.

Marcus was standing beside his motorcycle when I arrived. He swept me into a hug and bent me backward with passion. Just like his lovemaking, his greetings were never ordinary.

"Ready to go?"

"Where are we going?" I asked though I would follow him blindly.

"I thought you might like to have a front-row seat to a little natural beauty tonight," Marcus said, picking me up as if I weighed nothing at all, setting me on the motorcycle and handing me the helmet he bought just for when he rode with me.

He climbed on in front and revved the engine. Whenever we sped along the streets, I felt as if the street corners and people flying by were my past, sailing away without a trace. Marcus made it appear as if we were the only humans in existence. I was pleased to let him do exactly that.

I craned my neck, looking straight up at the hundreds of stories towering over us when finally, we stopped in front of a high rise.

"One of your father's buildings?"

"Yup," Marcus said, swinging his leg over the motorcycle before helping me off. "Office building that doubles as the best location for sunset in the city."

We took the elevator to the top of the building, our lips scarcely separating the entire ride. When we arrived at the top floor, Marcus pushed open the glass door that opened up onto a patio. The space was complete with cushioned furniture, a fire pit, and umbrellas. I walked to the edge, looking out at the horizon just as it began to turn colors. Marcus wrapped his arms around me, pressing into me from the back.

I exhaled, savoring the feeling of Marcus close to me and the brilliance of the sunset, my eyes and heart drinking in every moment. It took almost a full minute for me to realize that Marcus wasn't looking at the sunset, but at me. I turned my head, chuckling.

"What?"

He shook his head, continuing to gaze at me. I laughed as he took my hand to twirl me to the music.

Marcus leaned close to my ear, nestling his face into the side of my neck.

"When can I take you to meet my family?" he whispered.

My insides tightened at the thought. This step seemed so

momentous, but if we were going to share our lives, family time was inevitable.

"Whenever you like," I said.

"This weekend," Marcus decided, his eyes shut as he turned me toward him, cradling my head for a kiss.

"You'll have to come with me to see Saul too," I said. Marcus wasn't listening anymore as his hands ran up and down my body. He acted as if his hunger was insatiable and he might tear my clothes off at any moment. Though I wouldn't have objected, the ringing of my cell phone stopped us.

It was Saul. "One second."

"Of course, darling."

I took a couple of steps away from the rail. "Hey, Saul." "Hey. How are you feeling, Samantha?" "Better, thanks."

"Good," Saul said. "How was work today?"

"Fine. Got a lot done."

"Are you still there?"

I glanced over at Marcus. "No."

"With Marcus?" As always, Saul had his ways of knowing.

"Yes."

"Haven't seen him since the charity ball," Saul remarked. "Why don't you invite him over to the house for dinner tomorrow night? Does that work for you?"

He already knew it would. "Yes, of course. See you then."

I hung up, turning back to Marcus. He'd met Saul before, but somehow it still felt as if this were the first big "meeting the parents" moment. "Looks like you're up first," I teased. "Saul wants us to come over for dinner tomorrow night."

"I'm ready."

I walked into his arms again. I believed him. I would believe anything he said.

It was astonishing, the length of planning Marcus had gone to make this evening unforgettable. Between the sunset and the music, played by his dear friend Elton, the atmosphere exuded romance. We danced late into the night. After dedicating a final ballad called "Your Song" to us, Elton came over to chat.

"I've never seen Marcus so happy and relaxed," he said. "We have known each other for a long time. I can recall back to when the skirts chased him all over Europe. Oh, how they cried after he went home."

Marcus gave him an arrogant grin, which Elton responded to with a slap on the back. They obviously shared many secrets, none of which I cared to know.

Elton and I indulged in a last glass of wine while the crew cleared the equipment. I will forever remember that night as perfect. I was beginning to understand that love came in various forms and maybe this was true love.

I'd never had much of a flair for chess, but the heated post-dinner game that ensued between Marcus and Saul was more enjoyable than expected. I loved watching Marcus's handsome brow tense as he studied the chessboard. I fantasized about the feeling of his hands on me when he picked up his brandy glass to take a sip.

After laboring over the game for nearly two hours, Saul finally dealt a fatal blow, bringing the game to a checkmate.

Marcus sat back, a sound of competitive frustration escaped his throat.

"You're not an easy one to beat," Saul remarked in mild consolation. He sent me a wink of approval when Marcus looked away to take a drink.

"I'd like to believe that sir, but I'm afraid you're only trying to soothe my pride," Marcus said with a chuckle.

Saul laughed. "Maybe. There's still time for a rematch. Why don't we let this round be the judge?" Marcus smiled, good-natured determination lighting his eyes once more as he agreed. Was this what it felt like to abide in a relationship built on love, security, and support?

Now that I had tasted such a sensation, I couldn't imagine entering into another union without it. I sat back, sipping on my second glass of wine as Marcus and Saul set up the board for another game.

As I watched them tuck back into the game, I wondered if Saul's hints throughout the years that Joseph was not the one for me had all been leading up to this. Saul always seemed to know things. Perhaps he knew that Marcus was the man for me. Deep down, I was certainly starting to think so.

The day had arrived. It was my turn to meet the parents.

Marcus's family was tribe-like. His father was his European mother's senior by 20 years. They met in her modeling days, and John Marcus was instantly smitten.

He was mature, rough, and exiled by the elites. New York City's high society did not accept John Marcus on account of his shady business practices. They thought he was calculating and unacceptable. He had grown tired of business as usual and began to favor unorthodox methods of getting the job done. This lifestyle left the family vulnerable, so he kept security around them at all times. Family was everything to John Marcus. He had lost his father in a construction accident, buried alive on the job. This made him careful with the lives of his own family.

Once John Marcus had married Isabella and became the father of Marcus, his lifestyle became tame and far more socially acceptable. Isabella wanted to attend galas and soirees. Isabella's every wish was granted by John Marcus. He donated to every charity, campaign, and because that would land the family in the good graces of high society. He actively participated wherever was needed, and one day nearly all ill will had faded.

John Marcus was still a businessman which is why he hired my firm. These days he left the attorneys to handle any dirty work the company needed to clean up.

John was busy raising his twin daughters, Marcus's little sisters. They were 24 years old and twice the handful their brother was. Their father had tried to place them in top schools around the country, but their latest dream was to travel through

Europe, alone.

I was going with Marcus to meet everyone at the Poconos family lodge. The purpose of the ski vacation was to talk some sense into the twins.

"Are you ready to meet my sisters, sweetheart?" Marcus asked as we pulled up to the lodge. "It's our mission to talk them out of Europe. Dad thinks they're too young."

Concern started to worm its way across my face. "Marcus, maybe this isn't a good time to meet your family. Sounds like this might be private."

"Sam, darling, it's never private. You are going to have to get used to it. There is always something going on, especially with my sisters. Who knows, maybe you can offer some fresh perspective."

The tension in my face eased.

"Paige and Penelope are going to love you."

We had a wonderful time skiing with the family, soaking in the hot tub, playing cards with the twins.

Heated debates over Europe took place. The girls wanted a year away, John Marcus nothing at all, and Marcus suggested a summer. The compromise of a summer triumphed with the additional promise of heavy security. When their father looked away, Marcus tugged on his sisters' braids. His way of saying, "You're Welcome."

Marcus and I made love every night, but not at our usual volume. Quiet, yet passionate. Marcus laughed every time I kept him from making noise. One night, he pinned my hands down and whispered, "Seriously, do you think my parents are celibate? Baby, us Matthews' men are built to last."

Chapter 10

I lay in Marcus's bed, trying hard to fight the waves of sickness I felt coming on. The flu had been traveling through the office and I'd done everything I could to avoid it. My attempts at evading the virus had failed. I wasn't in the mood for sex and I would tell Marcus once he finished in the bathroom.

Undeniably, there was more to my emotional fragility and ill feelings than just the onset of the flu. Spending time with Marcus's family, seeing how he interacted with Saul, and becoming completely absorbed in our lovemaking had rocketed me to new heights. Nevertheless, Joseph was still present in my mind. Though the pain from his betrayal was diminishing, I had a nagging desire to call him. I couldn't help myself. Rick had intercepted his attempts to contact me for so long, but I needed closure. I needed to talk to him.

Marcus exited the bathroom. I could already see the fire in his eyes as he burned for me. I regretted the fact that I was going to have to tell him I was too sick to perform our usual, violently passionate rituals. He nuzzled my neck, stopping with a growl when his phone rang. He cursed under his breath as he reached for it.

"Damn it. Sorry, Samantha, I have to take this. I'll be back."

The moment he left the room, all of the self-control I had seemed to wash away instantly, and I knew what I had to do. I picked up the phone to call Joseph.

When he answered, the pain shot through me again.

"How are you my darling?" Joseph drawled. "I want to see you, Samantha. I want to see how you are."

"Joseph, I cannot see you yet. I still want you too much. Soon, please. Do not tell me anything about your marriage-"

Marcus came into the room. He appeared oblivious to my discomfort as he came straight toward me. His touch failed to ignite the heat within my body the way it usually did. No doubt the lingering thoughts of Joseph and the echoing of his voice were to blame for that.

He kissed me tenderly and held me. "Samantha, you are very easy to love. I am in love with you. So, take your time, But I will have your love and maybe your heart." He pressed on, "I have to go to Spain. Come with me."

"I can't right now," I replied in shock. "I have neglected my work. I need to get caught up and I think I have the flu. Plus, I am due to meet with Saul."

Marcus whispered words in my ears in an attempt to convince me to go with him. His voice remained soft and loving even amidst my rejection. Though I hadn't had the chance to tell him that I wasn't feeling well, Marcus seemed to know and made love to me without demand until I drifted off to sleep.

By the time I reached the sitting room where I was to meet Saul, my head was spinning and my stomach rumbled with unease.

Saul stood when I entered the room. He said a few words of greeting, but I couldn't make them out, so distracting was the queasiness I couldn't seem to push aside.

"I need to sit down," I finally managed.

"Of course," he said, leading me to the sofa.

"Samantha, I hope you don't mind, but Dr. Rae is in the other room and I have asked him to take a look at you."

All-knowing Saul, at it again.

"No, Saul, it isn't necessary," I retorted, wanting nothing more than to just lie down.

Saul put a hand up to stop my words. "I insist. You don't look well Samantha and if you are coming down with something it's best we catch it early. Why don't you lie down for a moment and I'll call him?"

I was happy to oblige. I felt so queasy. It didn't feel like the flu, it was something else. I'd felt this way once a long time ago.

Dr. Rae worked quickly. It wasn't long before I was given the reason why my symptoms felt distantly familiar. I was 12 weeks pregnant.

My eyes shot to Saul the moment Dr. Rae voiced the words I was hearing for the second time in my life. Joseph...I had to tell him...And Marcus...

Not a single hint of surprise registered on Saul's face as if he already knew.

www.ingramcontent.com/pod-product-compliance
Lightning Source LLC
Chambersburg PA
CBHW071237020426
42333CB00015B/1508